I WAS JUST WONDERING

I
Was
Just
Wondering

Philip Yancey

revised edition

WILLIAM B. EERDMANS PUBLISHING COMPANY
GRAND RAPIDS, MICHIGAN / CAMBRIDGE, U.K.

STRAND PUBLISHING
NARARA, NSW, AUSTRALIA

Published 1989
Paperback edition 1990
Revised edition 1998

Published jointly 1998 by
Wm. B. Eerdmans Publishing Co.
255 Jefferson Ave. S.E., Grand Rapids, Michigan 49503 /
P.O. Box 163, Cambridge CB3 9PU U.K.
and in Australia and New Zealand by
Strand Publishing
13 Strand Avenue, Narara, NSW, 2250, Australia

Printed in the United States of America

03 02   7

Library of Congress Cataloging-in-Publication Data

Yancey, Philip.
    I was just wondering / Philip Yancey.
        p.   cm.
    Rev. ed.
    ISBN 0-8028-4612-2 (pbk.)
    1. Christian life. I. Title.
BV4501.2.Y315   1998
    230 — dc21   98-29874
                                                CIP

For Harold Myra,
mentor and friend

Contents

Foreword

I suppose every writer worries about the inherent arrogance of the writing act. Every time I take up a pen (or, rather, remove the cover from my computer keyboard), I hope to produce something that will prove worth your time. I presume the right to cause you to put down whatever you are doing and pay attention to me. What gives me that right?

The longer I write, though, the less I worry about that question. I have learned that all I offer, all that any writer can offer, is a point of view. I present my own point of view — subjective, biased, personal, necessarily incomplete — and you the reader must determine whether the result merits your attention.

Five hundred years ago the Renaissance scholar Pico

della Mirandola delivered his famous "Oration on the Dignity of Man," which defined the role of humanity in creation. After God had created the animals, all the essential roles had been filled, but "the Divine Artificer still longed for some creature which might comprehend the meaning of so vast an achievement, which might be moved with love at its beauty and smitten with awe at its grandeur." To contemplate and appreciate all the rest, to reflect on meaning, to share in the power and exuberance of creativity, to revere and to hallow — these were the roles reserved for the species made in God's image.

Pico della Mirandola used exalted language, but as a writer I accept his premise. I look around me at the vast achievement at creation, and I want to express my own sense of awe and even love. The writer of faith, said Flannery O'Connor, the Christian writer, "will feel found by God to be worth dying for."

$$* \quad * \quad *$$

In 1983, when the editors of *Christianity Today* asked me to write a monthly column, my first concern was whether I would run out of things to write about. I was more accustomed to book projects, in which I pursued the same topic for several years. Could I adjust my range of vision fast enough each month?

Over the years, the anxiety has faded, and now the day I write my column is one of the most enjoyable of any month. I make it a point not to select a topic or theme until the due date arrives. The quick cycle of idea/writing/publication/reader-response seems almost therapeutic. It helps alleviate the isolation and paranoia that can come from long-term writing projects, in which feedback is separated from the writing process by several years.

Because of my own limited tolerance for books that are collections of reprinted material, I have worked to fit these columns into some sort of coherent organization. I was surprised to find certain themes recurring. Writing is like therapy: both processes bring into light what may otherwise stay hidden.

I learn about myself, in fact, as I look back over my own writing. These short pieces were all composed when I lived in downtown Chicago. I have since moved to Colorado, and you may well sense the longing for wildness and natural beauty that beckoned me there. I feel most comfortable alone, on a summer day, hiking up a 14,000-foot mountain with none but the marmots and pikas to keep me company.

Human beings, including myself, seem odd to me. Half-animal, half-angel, we keep surprising and disappointing ourselves and each other. As I write about people, I find myself homing in on the sense of irony that almost defines our species.

Though I am a Christian, and write frequently about my faith, I have never worn "the church" easily. I keep squirming inside it and making adjustments, trying to make a wrong-sized jacket fit. Growing up in an angry, fundamentalist church, I learned not to accept the party line. Now as a writer, those criticisms are turned back on me: If you can't believe them, what can you believe? I struggle with that question.

Often I use short pieces, like my column, as "scouting expeditions" for ideas that eventually take shape in fuller form. My reflections on "the midnight church" made it into the book *Church: Why Bother;* I continued pondering Simon Wiesenthal's question in *What's So Amazing about Grace;* the subjects of other columns found lengthier expresson in *Disappointment with God* and *The Jesus I Never Knew.*

In preparation for this book, I also read through a boxful of letters — every letter, in fact, that *Christianity Today* has received in response to my columns. You can probably guess which columns generated the most heat: anything touching on politics or sexuality. However, the single column which provoked the largest volume of mail was one that consisted entirely of questions.

I wrote that column just after reading Walker Percy's splendid book *The Message in the Bottle,* which begins with a series of questions, six pages of questions in all, along the lines of the following:

"Why does man feel so sad in the twentieth century?

"Why is a man apt to feel bad in a good environment, say suburban Short Hills, New Jersey, on an ordinary Wednesday afternoon? Why is the same man apt to feel good in a very bad environment, say an old hotel on Key Largo during a hurricane?

"Why is it that the only time I ever saw my uncle happy during his entire life was the afternoon of December 7, 1941, when the Japanese bombed Pearl Harbor?"

Percy's interrogative style triggered some of my own questions, and I devoted a whole column to that list, without attempting any answers. Frankly, I think it a healthy sign that the readers of *Christianity Today* had such enthusiasm for a column full of questions. Their reaction led me to the form around which this book is organized — a book of many questions and a few answers.

There's one last question I never got around to. Why do so few Christians read Walker Percy?

Philip Yancey

Part I

The Human Animal

Why are there so many kinds of animals? Couldn't the world get along with, say, 300,000 species of beetles instead of 500,000? What good are they?

Why is it that the most beautiful animals on earth are hidden away from all humans except those wearing elaborate SCUBA equipment? Who are they beautiful for?

Why is almost all religious art realistic, whereas much of God's creation — zebra, swallowtail butterfly, crystalline structure — excels at abstract design?

Why are dogs so much easier to train than cats? Why are African elephants almost impossible to train? Which does God take most pride in, a dog or a cat?

Are human beings animals? Are they anything but animals? Why aren't human beings easier to train?

Why are there dirty jokes? What makes the physiology of excretion and reproduction so funny anyhow?

As Walker Percy asks, "Why does man feel so sad in the twentieth century? Why does man feel so bad in the very age when, more than in any other age, he has succeeded in satisfying his needs and making over the world for his own use?"

Do gorillas and aardvarks go through a mid-life crisis?

Why is Ecclesiastes in the Bible? Was its author going through a mid-life crisis? What would a mid-life crisis look like in an ancient Hebrew king?

Why did Solomon, who showed such wisdom in writing proverbs, spend the last years of his life breaking all those proverbs?

Why is the Song of Solomon in the Bible? Why is the Song of Solomon, alone of all biblical books, interpreted allegorically when in fact the Bible gives no clue of any allegorical intent? How did a religion that includes a book like the Song of Solomon among its sacred writings get branded as an enemy of sex?

Why is sex fun?

I was just wondering.

The Universe and My Aquarium

When I look out my downtown window I see a twelve-story apartment building, all concrete and glass, its balconies speckled with a random assortment of bicycles, Weber grills, and lawn chairs. Closer, I see twisted metal antennae growing like bare branches from a video store, the pebbly gray roof of a Donut shop, the aluminum exhaust vent from an Italian restaurant, and a web of black wires to bring electricity to all these monuments of civilization. (We didn't choose this place for the view.)

But if I turn my head to the right, as I often do, I can watch a thriving tropical paradise. A piece of the Caribbean has snuck into my study. A glass rectangle contains five seashells coated with velvety algae, stalks of coral planted like shrubbery in the gravel bottom, and seven creatures as exotic as any that exist on God's earth. Salt water fish have colors so pure and lustrous that it seems the fish themselves are actively creating the hues, rather than merely reflecting light waves to produce them. The most brightly colored fish in my aquarium is split in half, with a glowing yellow tail and a shocking magenta head, as if he had stuck his head in a paint bucket.

My tastes tend toward the bizarre, and in addition to beautiful fish, I have two that are startling but hardly beautiful. A long-horned cowfish — so named because of the horns extending from his head and abdomen — propels his boxy body around the tank with impossibly small side fins. If a bumblebee defies aerodynamics, the cowfish defies aquatics. Another, a lion fish, is all fins and spikes and menacing protuberances, like one of those gaudy paper creatures that dance across the stage in Chinese opera.

I keep the aquarium as a reminder. When writer's loneliness sets in, or suffering hits too close, or the gray of Chicago's sky and buildings blankets my mind and moods, I turn and gaze. There are no Rocky Mountains out my window, and the nearest blue whale is half a continent away, but I do have this small rectangle to remind me of the larger world outside. Half a million species of beetles, ten thousand wild butterfly designs, a billion fish just like mine poking around in coral reefs — a lot of beauty is going on out there, often unobserved by human eyes. My aquarium reminds me.

Yet even here, in the beauty of my artificial universe, suffering thrives as well. Nature, said Chesterton, is our *sister*, not our mother; she too has fallen. The spikes and fins on my lion fish are appropriately menacing; they can contain enough toxin to kill a person. And when any one fish shows a sign of weakness, the others will turn on it, tormenting without mercy. Just last week the other six fish were brutally attacking the infected eye of the cowfish. In aquariums, pacifists die young.

I spend much time and effort fighting off the parasites, bacteria, and fungi that invade the tank. I run a portable chemical laboratory to test the specific gravity, nitrate and nitrite levels, and ammonia content. I pump in vitamins and antibiotics and sulfa drugs, and enough enzymes to make a rock grow. I filter the water through glass fibers and charcoal and expose it to an ultraviolet light. Even so, the fish don't last long. Fish are dubious pets, I tell my friends; their only "tricks" are eating, getting sick, and dying.

You would think, in view of all this energy expended on their behalf, that my fish would at least be grateful. Not so. Every time my shadow appears above the tank, they dive for cover into the nearest shell. Three times a day I open the lid and drop in food, yet they respond to each opening as a sure sign of my designs to torture them. Fish are not affirming pets.

The arduous demands of aquarium management have taught me a deep appreciation for what is involved in running a universe based on dependable physical laws. To my fish I am deity, and one who does not hesitate to intervene. I balance the salts and trace elements in their water. No food enters their tank unless I retrieve it from my freezer and drop it in. They would not live a day without the electrical gadget that brings oxygen to the water.

Whenever I must treat an infection, I face an agonizing choice. Ideally, I should move the infected fish to a quarantine tank in order to keep the others from pestering it and to protect them from contagion. But such violent intervention in the tank, the mere act of chasing the sick fish with the net, could do more damage than the infection. Stress resulting from the treatment itself may actually cause death.

I often long for a way to communicate with those small-brained water-dwellers. Out of ignorance, they perceive me as a constant threat. I cannot convince them of my true concern. I am too large for them, my actions too incomprehensible. My acts of mercy they see as cruelty; my attempts at healing they view as destruction. To change their perceptions would require a form of incarnation.

I bought my aquarium to brighten a dull room, but ended up learning a few lessons about running a universe. Maintaining one requires constant effort and a precarious balancing of physical laws. Often the most gracious acts go unnoticed or even cause resentment. As for direct intervention, that is never simple, in universes large or small.

Endangered Wildness

In what she later called "the most transporting pleasure of my life on the farm," Isak Dinesen went flying across the unspoiled plains of Africa with her friend Denys Finch-Hatton. In the film version of *Out of Africa*, the character playing Denys offers to show "the world as God sees it," and, indeed, the next few minutes of cinematography come close to presenting exactly that. As the frail Moth airplane soars beyond the escarpment marking the beginning of Kenya's Rift Valley, the ground falls abruptly away and the camera captures a glimpse of Eden in the grasslands just below.

Great herds of zebras scatter at the sound of the motor, each group wheeling in unison, as if a single mind controlled the bits of modern art dashing across the plain.

Huge giraffes — they seemed so gangly and awkward when standing still — lope away with exquisite gracefulness. Spry gazelles, bounding past the larger animals, fill in the edges of the scene.

The world as God sees it — does that phrase merely express some foamy Romantic notion or does it contain truth? The Bible gives intriguing hints. Proverbs tells of the act of Creation when Wisdom "was the craftsman at his [God's] side . . . filled with delight day after day . . . rejoicing in his whole world." The seraphs in Isaiah's vision who declared "the whole earth is full of his glory" could hardly have been referring to human beings — not if the rest of the book of Isaiah is to be believed. At least God had the glory of Nature then, during that dark period when Israel faced extinction and Judah slid toward idolatry.

God makes most plain how he feels about the animal kingdom in his longest single speech, a magnificent address found at the end of Job. Look closely and you will notice a common thread in the specimens he holds up for Job's edification:

- A lioness hunting her prey.
- A mountain goat giving birth in the wilds.
- A rogue donkey roaming the salt flats.
- An ostrich flapping her useless wings with joy.
- A stallion leaping high to paw the air.
- A hawk, an eagle, and a raven building their nests on the rocky crags.

That's a mere warmup — Zoology 101 in Job's education. From there God advances to the behemoth, a hippo-like creature no one can tame, and the mighty, dragonish leviathan. "Can you make a pet of him like a bird or put him on a leash for your girls?" God asks with a touch of sarcasm. "The mere sight of him is overpowering. No one is fierce enough to rouse him. Who then is able to stand against me?"

Wildness is God's underlying message to Job, the one trait his menagerie all share. God is celebrating those members of his created world who will never be domesticated by human beings. Evidently, wild animals serve an essential function in "the world as God sees it." They bring us down a notch, reminding us of something we'd prefer to forget: our creatureliness. And they also announce to our senses the splendor of an invisible, untameable God.

*   *   *

Several times a week I run among such wild animals, unmolested, for I run through the Lincoln Park Zoo in downtown Chicago. I have gotten to know them well, as charming neighbors, but I always make a mental effort to project them into their natural states.

Three rock hopper penguins neurotically pace back and forth on a piece of concrete sprayed to look like ice. I envision them free, hopping from ice floe to ice floe in Antarctica, surrounded by millions of their comic-faced cousins.

An ancient elephant stands against a wall, keeping time three ways: his body sways from side to side to one beat, his tail marks a different rhythm entirely, and his trunk moves up and down to yet a third. I struggle to imagine this sluggish giant exciting terror in an African forest.

And the paunchy cheetah flopped across a rock shelf — could this animal possibly belong to the species that can, on a short course, out-accelerate a Porsche?

It requires a huge mental leap for me to place the penguin, elephant, and cheetah back where they belong, where they came from. Somehow God's stirring message about wildness evaporates among the moats and bars and plastic educational placards of the zoo. Yet, I am fortunate to live near the zoo. Otherwise, Chicago would offer up only squirrels, pigeons, cockroaches, rats, and a stray songbird. Is this what God had in mind when he granted Adam dominion?

*   *   *

It is hard to avoid a sermonic tone when writing about wild animals, for our sins against them are very great. In recent years the elephant population has been reduced by half, and rhinos nearly made exinct, thanks mainly to poachers and rambunctious soldiers with machine guns. And every year we are destroying an area of rain forest — and all its animal residents — equal in size to all of New England.

Most wildlife writing focuses on these vanishing animals themselves, but I find myself wondering about the ultimate impact on us. What else, besides that innate appreciation for wildness, have we lost? Could distaste for authority, or even a loss of God-awareness, derive in part from this atrophied sense? God's mere mention of the animals struck a chord of awe in Job; what about us, who grow up tossing peanuts across the moat to the behemoths and leviathans?

Naturalist John Muir, who never lost a vision for "the world as God sees it," concluded sadly, "it is a great comfort . . . that vast multitudes of creatures, great and small and infinite in number, lived and had a good time in God's love before man was created."

The heavens declare the glory of God; and so do breaching whales and pronking springboks. Fortunately, in some corners of the world vast multitudes of creatures can still live and have a good time in God's love. The least we could do is make room for them — for our sakes as well as theirs.

Winter Luxuries

"April is the cruelest month," begins *The Waste Land*, one of this century's most famous poems. T. S. Eliot may be a great poet, but that line tends to puzzle those of us who live in the tundra belt. April cruel? That's the month we rediscover grass and find that water can be soft and wet again, the month when trees finally remember they're supposed to have leaves. If you're talking cruel, what of January or February?

That's the official northern wisdom, anyway. Having spent the first half of my life in Atlanta, and the next portion in Chicago, I'm unconvinced. Yes, we complain about the cold, and talk of winters past in hushed, reproachful tones; but I'm half-convinced we're bluffing. I

14

think we secretly love the season and feel a twinge of sadness when spring arrives.

I've noticed, for example, that people seem cheeriest on days most frigid. At bus stops, we actually talk to one another! Granted, we mumble incomprehensibly through breath-frosted scarves, and our conversations encompass only one subject — the cold — but at least we're talking. Walk into any grocery or hardware store and you can instantly provoke a lively conversation with just four words: "It's freezing out there!"

"It was so cold in my pantry that the ketchup bottle froze solid." "Tried to get my dog outside this morning. She took one sniff and made a beeline for the electric blanket." "I heard the difference between forty below and thirty below is that your spit freezes before it hits the ground." That's the kind of talk you will likely hear in Chicago or International Falls or Bismarck in mid-January.

In winter we have a common enemy so powerful that it rearranges our priorities: newscasters swap stories about the cold for five minutes before they get to such "lesser" matters as international conflicts and world trade. Our real opponent is outside, palpably surrounding us, and we humans are huddled together behind barriers of plaster and brick; and we're *surviving*. Together, we are going to beat that enemy. The spirit is eerily atavistic: We are warriors in a cave, trying to work up courage against the herd of mammoths outside.

I heard recently about a poll of senior citizens in London. To the question, "What was the happiest time of your life?" sixty percent answered, "The Blitz." Every

night squadrons of Luftwaffe bombers would dump
tons of explosives on the city, reducing a proud civilization to rubble — and now the victims recall that time
with nostalgia! They, too, had a common enemy outside,
and huddled together in dark places, determined to
survive.

*   *   *

People used to use a strange, humble expression: they
would talk about being at the "mercy" of the elements.
With all our technological defenses, we are rarely at their
mercy anymore, and rarely humble. Thanks to me-
teorology, weather has even lost its surprise factor. (Why
is it that television weathermen drone on about jet
streams and draw arrows all over the globe when all I
want to know is what coat to wear tomorrow?) But every
once in a while, in January or February, we get a fine,
unruly blast of cold and snow that stops us, literally, in
our tracks, and teaches us about "mercy." Winter, above
all, offers a reminder of creaturehood. Once more we see
ourselves as tiny, huddling creatures dependent on each
other and on the God who created the awesome universe.

"God's voice thunders in marvelous ways," said
Elihu to Job. "He says to the snow, 'Fall on the earth,' and
to the rain shower, 'Be a mighty downpour.' So that all
men he has made may know his work, he stops every
man from his labor." It happens even in a great city like
Chicago. On the day of the big blizzard, the trains cease
running, cross-country skiers replace cars on the streets,
and everyone stops from labor.

*   *   *

One day in February I drove south along Chicago's Lake
Shore Drive toward downtown. The sun was shining brilliantly — oddly, it always does on the coldest days, for it
is the cloud cover that holds in the earth's heat. On my
left, Lake Michigan was deciding whether or not to freeze.
Just above the turquoise water line, ice fog was forming,
that startling phenomenon in which water, skipping in-
termediate stages, condenses directly into ice crystals. On
my right, Chicago's skyline was lit by the softened,
slanted rays of winter sun. In a curious sort of way, the
whole scene seemed *friendly*. I couldn't understand why
until I noticed the puffs of pure white smoke wafting from
the top of each building. It was as if they were breathing
— even concrete and steel had taken on something of an
organic quality.

Maybe Eliot was right about April being the cruelest
month: it puts an end to the subtle delights of winter. I
had thoughts along this line as I drove down Lake Shore
Drive, until I turned in to Lincoln Park. And there I saw
some of Chicago's homeless. As barriers against the cold,
they had only a few layers of old newspapers and some
plastic bags. They, too, huddled together, but there was
little of the joy and camaraderie I had sensed from people
at bus stops and in grocery stores. These folks were just
trying to stay alive.

It was then I realized that enjoying February, using
words like *refreshing* and *invigorating*, sensing the friend-
liness of a man-made redoubt against the elements —
these were the greatest of luxuries. It was then I realized
another, essential meaning to the word *mercy*. A sense of

creaturehood — huddling together in caves or bomb shelters or Chicago buildings — produces a feeling like joy
only if we the creatures show "mercy" to each other. It is
a good lesson to remember — in February, April, or any
other month.

A Theology from Dirty Jokes

C. S. Lewis had the literary gift of one-liners. His tongue lodged securely in cheek, he once said something like this: In the absence of any other evidence, the essentials of natural theology could be argued from the human phenomena of dirty jokes and attitudes toward death.

Let's start with dirty jokes. They dwell almost exclusively on the subjects of excretion and reproduction, two of the most "natural" processes on earth; yet in our smirks and double entendres we treat them as utterly unnatural, even comical. Functions which we share with all other animals somehow, to humans alone, seem strange. Try to envision a horse or cow bashful about the need to excrete in public. Or imagine a dog or cat with sexual hangups, reluctant to mate.

As for death, man acts even less animal-like in its presence. Nature treats death as a normal, everyday occurrence. An octopus lays a million eggs to produce one surviving offspring. Flies, buzzards, bacteria, and all carnivores build their careers around the fact of death. Only we humans treat it with shock and revulsion, as though we can't get used to the reality, universal though it may be. Every culture devises elaborate ceremonies to mark the final passage of a human being. Even those of us in the Christian West, with our traditional belief in an afterlife, dress up our corpses in new suits, embalm them (for what, posterity?), and bury them in airtight caskets and concrete vaults to slow natural decay. In these rituals we act out a stubborn reluctance to yield to this most powerful of human experiences.

Lewis suggests that these anomalies (like the more commonly cited human conscience) betray a permanent state of *disunity* within human beings. An individual person is a spirit made in the image of God but merged with a body of mortal flesh. Dirty jokes and an obsession with death express a rumbling sense of discord about this in-between state. We *should* feel dissonance; we are, after all, immortals trapped in mortal surroundings. We lack unity because long ago a gap fissured open between our mortal and immortal parts; theologians trace the fault line back to the Fall.

Not everyone, of course, subscribes to this natural theology. Modern-day biologists, psychologists, and anthropologists operate from a materialistic assumption that denies the spirit. They study our mortal parts and conclude there is nothing more. (Materialists, said Tolstoy, mistake that which limits life for life itself.) But don't these observers have some explaining to do? I have yet to see an evolutionary psychologist's paper postulating the origin of dirty jokes. What function do they serve in perpetuating a gene pool? Whence come these stirrings of dissonance?

According to the biblical view of humanity, it is *natural* that we blush at excretion and draw back from death. Such actions seem odd because they *are* odd. In all of earth there are no exact parallels of spirit and immortality housed in matter. The discomfiture we feel may be our most accurate human sensation, reminding us we are not quite "at home" here. C. S. Lewis used hyperbole: one would be hard pressed to derive most essential theology from dirty jokes and our attitudes toward death. But one might be harder pressed to deny all natural theology in the face of these and other rumors of transcendence.

In addition to these oddities of human nature, Lewis mentioned one more: our startled reactions to the concept of time. The last page of *Reflections on the Psalms* summarizes the transitory, suspended state we live in.

> We are so little reconciled to time that we are even astonished at it. "How he's grown!" we exclaim, "How time flies!" as though the universal form of our experience were again and again a novelty. It is as strange as if a fish were repeatedly surprised at the wetness of water. And that would be strange indeed; unless of course the fish were destined to become, one day, a land animal.

High School Reunion

If I were a diehard evolutionist seeking to discredit the Christian doctrine of man, I think I would spend my time not digging for bones in Dr. Leakey's Africa, but rather roaming the halls of America's high schools. They offer science a showcase for "the human animal" at its most atavistic. I say that having just returned from my twentieth-year high school reunion.

At no other time in life does the principle "biology is destiny" seem to apply with such force as in the teenage years. I found that, some twenty years after high school, the group we called "jocks" still walked with a peculiar swagger, despite their potbellies and receding hairlines. Another group, cheerleaders, were the best preserved. Having learned early on that flesh — face and body —

was their best ticket to success, they thus disguised facial wrinkles and extra pounds better than anyone else. In stocking feet, rather sheepishly, those career women and housewives led us all in half-remembered high school cheers.

The nerds made an appearance too. In high school these bookish types won the science fair awards, led the chess club to victory, and raised the school's level of SAT scores, gaining for their efforts universal abuse and scorn. The passage of time has granted them a measure of revenge: from such adolescent raw material have emerged research scientists, computer programmers, and stock market whizzes.

One high school grouping has gone through mutations in the last twenty years, from "hood" to greaser to punk. None came to the reunion with hair slathered in butch wax or wearing a white T-shirt with a cigarette pack rolled up in the sleeve. But the former hoods still huddled together on the sidelines, the radical fringe on society's stiff upper lip. Only the styles, not the roles, had changed.

One of my most vivid high school memories involves a colossal clash between the number one hood (I suppose he would be a gang leader today) and the number one jock, the school quarterback. At least 300 students blocked off a hallway, keeping frantic teachers away, as the two duelled over a girlfriend.

I will never forget how abruptly the spirit of the cheering mob changed when the hood grabbed the quarterback and bashed his head against a sharp water fountain nozzle — once, two times, three times. The crowd melted away in sickened silence, letting teachers through at last to tend to the quarterback, now writhing on the floor in a widening pool of blood. The girl who had inspired the combat sat hunched in a tiny ball by a locker, sobbing.

*   *   *

A behaviorist could view that scene as the human version of Rocky Mountain sheep lowering their heads and colliding with a force that sends echoes through the canyons. The humans, like sheep, were establishing a tribal and sexual dominance, a status won through brute strength. But there is another side to the human animal. G. K. Chesterton said, "Man is not a balloon going up into the sky, nor a mole burrowing merely in the earth; but rather a thing like a tree, whose roots are fed from the earth, while its highest branches seem to rise almost to the stars." And Dostoevsky added, "Man is not an arithmetical expression; he is a mysterious and puzzling being, and his nature is extreme and contradictory all through." He was expressing the most basic fact of Christian anthropology, that the human animal was created to be more than animal.

As I reflected on my high school experience, it struck me that the gospel calls us to cast off the simple "biology is destiny" formula and to reach farther and higher toward spiritual reality. In short, we are asked to transcend biological destiny and prove that we are more than animals.

High school amply demonstrates the drive toward self-preservation, "survival of the fittest" at its most primal. Like animals, we compete on the basis of power and physical appearance. A beautiful face, a famous name, or an impressive physique can guarantee success, and exactly that kind of success is what schools reward so lavishly with homecoming crowns and sports trophies. High school shows what happens when, untrammeled by the polite artifice of "maturity," we express the base instincts we inherited as members of the human species.

But our Christian calling asks us to defy those instincts. Jesus announced a great reversal of values in his Sermon on the Mount, elevating not the rich or attractive, but rather the poor, the persecuted, and those who mourn. Instead of lauding such traits as wealth, political power, and physical beauty, he warned against their dangers. A passage like Luke 18 shows the kind of people who impressed Jesus: an oppressed widow, a despairing tax collector, a small child, a blind beggar.

Instinctually, animals mark the weak (the nerds?) for quick destruction; we are commanded to value them. We are also told that fulfillment comes not in the pursuit of happiness, but rather in the pursuit of service. We are asked to respond to our most grievous failures not by covering them up, but by repenting of them openly. When you are wronged, says the gospel, extend forgiveness, not vengeance. And don't hoard material things, but trade them all for the kingdom of heaven, a pearl of great price.

*   *   *

Christians have long worried that evolutionary theory might reduce humanity to a status lower than that the Bible assigns it. Our failure to convince many scientists of the *uniqueness* of humankind, made "in the image of God," makes me wonder about trying a different tack entirely. What if, instead of trying to prove that *homo sapiens* is not an animal, we sought to prove that we are far more? Instead of challenging the antiquity of fossils or disputing the results of genetic engineering, we could simply demonstrate that biology is not destiny. What would happen in the national consensus if these nine words came to mind when you said the word "Christian": love, joy, peace, patience, kindness, goodness, faithfulness, gentleness, and self-control?

I know for a fact that no one in my high school gave out awards for the nine qualities listed above, the biblical definition of "the fruit of the Spirit." But I believe that the effect of those qualities will endure long after all high school yearbooks have turned to dust, long after the solar system itself has grown cold and still. And perhaps, just perhaps, exhibiting the fruit of the Spirit may be our very best defense against a materialist view of humankind here on earth.

The New Determinism

If I hear the term "mid-life crisis" one more time, I may have one. In common parlance that phrase may encompass any struggle of the soul that occurs between the ages of 31 and 55. And if love covers a multitude of sins, the redoubtable mid-life crisis disguises a multitude of the same. People no longer commit adultery and break up their marriages; they go through mid-life crisis.

I have heard the same monologue from so many of my male friends that I may print up cue cards to save them the trouble of having to formulate fresh rationalizations. The code words go like this: "I have changed. I am a different man today than when I married her. I must be true to myself, and follow who I really am as far as that leads me. I can see why I used to love her, but I

am now bound to follow my new dreams and expectations, which she simply can't fulfill."

Often a hormonal complication gets mentioned: a
deep, abiding attraction to "another woman who truly
understands me" (coincidentally, she often happens to be
ten years younger and fifteen pounds lighter than the
wife). The husband earnestly recounts his struggle, his
facial muscles expressing a mixture of deep pain and
poignancy over "a force bigger than I that I simply cannot
resist." I try not to flinch when I hear that this experience
is wholly unexpected and unique, possibly something
new in the history of the world. (In truth, I feel like hand-
ing my friend a copy of *Anna Karenina*, which says everything worth saying about the "unique" experiences of
passion, love, boredom, selfishness, and lust.)

Because my care for my friends will endure despite
the outcome of their mid-life crises, I strive to be understanding, even when they ultimately reject my advice. But
after hearing the very same script three, four, and five
times, I must confess sheer bafflement at two trends. Although they seem utter enigmas to me, these trends keep
edging into my conversations about the mid-life crisis.

1. My friends spend much time looking inward, examining themselves in order to ascertain what will make
them fulfilled, self-actualized, happy (or whatever the
current buzzword happens to be). Does this not seem
odd? A self, the observer, scrutinizes a self, the observed,
which also happens to be the same self! How can I observe
myself to find out what I really want if I the observer am
the very one who is wanting it?

Maybe I am missing something here, but I have the
distinct impression that some *a priori* rules of logic are

being tossed aside. Modern physics has established with its Principle of Indeterminacy that the very fact of observing introduces distortions into the event observed, changing its nature. Philosophy and physics aside, can a person who is actively lusting objectively examine himself and decide the future direction of his life without being affected by the lust itself? That seems to me like asking an alcoholic to rationally assess his "need" for alcohol at a New Year's Eve party.

Reflecting on these matters, I have more appreciation for why the Bible avoids fuzzy psychologisms and says simply to the stealer, "Steal no more," and to the tempted, "Flee temptation." The Bible challenges us to look upward, not inward, for counsel at moments of crisis. As Jeremiah says, "The heart is deceitful above all things and beyond cure. Who can understand it?" Not very sophisticated-sounding advice, to be sure; but then some of our modern advice gets so sophisticated it soars beyond the realm of rational coherence.

2. Once the observing self learns what will make him happy, fulfilled, and actualized, a kind of determinism switches on. The husband feels *bound* to follow the inner voice assuring him that Miss B is the solution to his life, not timeworn Mrs. A. This determinism is a force of the highest order, and often proves more powerful than paternal instincts and marriage vows to state and God. With sad regularity we watch husbands and fathers (or wives and mothers) leave spouse, children, and perhaps church and faith, in order to follow this strange beckoning from within. "I *have* to," they say. "This is something bigger than I am. I cannot resist it."

Many of these same people would violently oppose

the notion of determinism or the merest hint of legalism. Their actions, for example, flout the Ten Commandments, which they may dismiss as restrictive and freedom-stifling. Yet what could be more deterministic than being bound to follow such intangibles as feelings, personality, predisposition, and magnetic attraction?

I hope some enlightened psychologists will give attention to what I consider a tyranny of psychological determinism. In the meantime, I hold up for consideration an appropriate analogy explored by Dorothy Sayers in *Begin Here*, an obscure book written during World War II. She resolves the dilemma this way:

> It is true that man is dominated by his psychological make-up, but only in the sense that an artist is dominated by his material. It is not possible for a sculptor to carve a filigree brooch out of granite; to that extent he is the servant of the stone he works in. His craftsmanship is good precisely in so far as he uses granite to express his artistic intentions in a manner conformable to the stone's own nature. This is no slavery, but the freedom of the sculptor and the freedom of the stone working together in harmony. The better the sculptor understands the true nature of his raw material, the greater is his freedom in using it; and so it is with every man, when he uses his own mind and emotions to express his conscious intention.

Sayers goes on to describe the difference between murdering one's mother-in-law and writing a detective story about such a murder. Both acts may spring from the same unconscious impulse, she says, so that each activity begins with the same raw material. But the difference lies precisely in how the unconscious impulse is acted upon.

We are getting better and better at identifying what Sayers calls "the raw material" of unconscious or subconscious impulses. Maybe it's time for an equally strong emphasis on the human freedom that allows us sometimes to act against that subconscious, for the sake of fidelity.

The Problem of Pleasure

Why is sex fun? Reproduction certainly doesn't require pleasure: some animals simply split in half to reproduce, and even humans use methods of artificial insemination that don't involve pleasure. Why, then, is sex fun?

Why is eating fun? Plants and the lower animals manage to obtain their quota of nutrients without the luxury of taste buds. Why can't we?

Why are there colors? Some people get along fine without the ability to detect color. Why complicate vision for all the rest of us?

Another question: What hubris drove our Founding Fathers to include the pursuit of happiness in a list of three inalienable rights? "We hold these truths to be self-evident," they said by way of explanation. Self-evident?

Considering the weight of history, how could anyone conceive of the pursuit of happiness as a self-evident, inalienable right? Death, maybe — no one can steal that from us — but the pursuit of happiness? On what basis do we take it for granted?

It struck me the other day, after I had read my umpteenth book on the problem of pain (the theological obsession of this century, it seems), that I have never even seen a book on "the problem of pleasure." Nor have I met a philosopher who goes around shaking his head in perplexity over the basic question of why we experience pleasure.

Where did pleasure come from? That seems to me a huge question — the philosophical equivalent, for atheists, to the problem of pain for Christians. On the issue of pleasure, Christians can breathe a little easier. A good and loving God would naturally want his creatures to experience delight, joy, and personal fulfillment. We Christians start from that assumption and then look for ways to explain the origin of suffering. But don't atheists and secular humanists have an equal obligation to explain the origin of pleasure in a world of randomness and meaninglessness?

One person, at least, faced the issue squarely. In his indispensable book *Orthodoxy*, G. K. Chesterton traced his own Christian conversion to the problem of pleasure. He found materialism too thin to account for the sense of wonder and delight that sometimes marks our response to the world, and especially to such simple human acts as sex, and childbirth, and artistic creation. Here is how he tells it:

> I felt in my bones, first that this world does not explain itself. . . . Second, I came to feel as if magic must have a

meaning, and meaning must have some one to mean it.
There was something personal in the world, as in a work
of art. . . . Third, I thought this purpose beautiful in its
old design, in spite of its defects, such as dragons. Fourth,
that the proper form of thanks to it is some form of humility and restraint: we should thank God for beer and Burgundy by not drinking too much of them. . . . And last,
and strangest, there had come into my mind a vague and
vast impression that in some way all good was a remnant
to be stored and held sacred out of some primordial ruin.
Man had saved his good as [Robinson] Crusoe saved his
goods: he had saved them from a wreck. All this I felt and
the age gave me no encouragement to feel it. And all this
time I had not even thought of Christian theology.

In a single sweep, Chesterton has helped clarify the
problem of pleasure. For the unbeliever, the problem centers in the question of origin: Where did pleasure come
from? Chesterton searched all alternatives, and settled on
Christianity as the only reasonable explanation for the
existence of pleasure in the world. Moments of pleasure
are remnants, like goods washed ashore from a ship-
wreck, like bits of Paradise extended through time.

But once a person has accepted that explanation, acknowledging God to be the source of all good gifts, new
problems stir up. The proper way to thank God for his good
gifts — and here teetotalers may take exception with
Chesterton's examples of beer and Burgundy — is by using
them with humility and restraint. It occurs to me that
perhaps I *have* read a book on the problem of pleasure: the
biblical book of Ecclesiastes. That story of decadence by the
richest, wisest, and most talented person in the world

serves as a perfect allegory for what can happen when we lose sight of the Giver whose good gifts we enjoy.

As Chesterton saw it, the sexual promiscuity described in a book like Ecclesiastes (its implied author had 700 wives and 300 concubines) is not so much an overvaluing of sex as a de-valuing. "To complain that I could only be married once was like complaining that I had only been born once. It was incommensurate with the terrible excitement of which one was talking. It showed, not an exaggerated sensibility to sex, but a curious insensibility to it. . . . Polygamy is a lack of the realization of sex; it is like a man plucking five pears in a mere absence of mind."

Thus pleasure is at once a great good and a grave danger. If we start chasing pleasure as an end in itself, along the way we may lose sight of the One who gave us such good gifts as sexual drive, taste buds, and the capacity to appreciate beauty. As Ecclesiastes tells it, a wholesale devotion to pleasure will, paradoxically, lead to a state of utter despair.

All of which leads me to consider a whole new approach to our society's decadence. Every Sunday I can turn on the radio or television and hear preachers decry the drugs, sexual looseness, greed, and crime that are "running rampant" in the streets of America. But rather than merely wag our fingers at such obvious abuses of God's good gifts, perhaps we should work at demonstrating to the world where good gifts actually come from, and why they are good. I think of the old adage, "Hypocrisy is the obeisance that vice gives to virtue": drug trips as obeisance to true beauty, promiscuity as obeisance to sexual fulfillment, greed as obeisance to stewardship, and crime a shortcut way to seize all the rest.

Somehow Christians have gotten a reputation as anti-pleasure, and this despite the fact that they believe pleasure was an invention of the Creator himself. We Christians have a choice. We can present ourselves as uptight bores who sacrificially forfeit half the fun of life by limiting our indulgence in sex, food, and other sensual pleasures. Or we can set about enjoying pleasure to the fullest, which means enjoying it in the way the Creator intended.

Not everyone will buy the Christian philosophy of pleasure. Some skeptics will scoff at any insistence on moderation with a "Pity you poor ignoramuses" attitude of condescension. For these skeptics, I have a few simple questions. Why is sex pleasurable? Why is eating fun? Why are there colors? I'm still waiting for a good explanation that does not include the word God.

Part II

In the World

Why are there so many alcoholics these days? Why don't they just come to church instead of sequestering themselves in their own gatherings? Why do sinners feel so attracted to Jesus but so repulsed by the church?

Why do persons with AIDS so often not come to church? Why did former Surgeon General Koop, an evangelical Christian, get so much hate mail from other evangelical Christians?

Why do virtually all instances of church discipline involve sexual sins? Why do I hear so few sermons on the sins of pride, greed, sloth, and gluttony? Would Christians support a national Prohibition movement against the major health hazard of obesity?

Why do so many hospitals have Christian-sounding names? Why do they function just like every other hospital? What would a truly Christian hospital look like?

Where did racial hatred come from? Where did races come from? Why didn't God make all people alike, like dandelions and hydrogen molecules?

Does God love Americans more than Iraqis and Libyans? Irish Protestants more than Irish Catholics?

Where do political tyrants come from? Why does God let them inflict such evil on the world? Why did God stay silent during the Holocaust?

The Midnight Church

I attended a unique "church" recently, one that manages, with no denominational headquarters or paid staff, to attract millions of devoted members each week. It goes by the name Alcoholics Anonymous. I went at the invitation of a friend, who had just confessed to me his problem with drinking. "Come along," he said, "and I think you'll catch a glimpse of what the early church must have been like."

At twelve o'clock on a Monday evening I entered a ramshackle house that had been used for six other sessions already that day. Acrid clouds of cigarette smoke hung like tear gas in the air. It didn't take long to sense what my friend had meant with his allusion to the early church. A well-known politician and several prominent millionaires were mixing freely with unemployed dropouts and kids who wore Band-Aids to hide the needle marks on their arms. The "sharing time" was like a textbook small group, marked by compassionate listening, warm responses, and many hugs. Introductions went like this: "Hi, I'm Tom, and I'm an alcoholic and a drug addict." Instantly everyone shouted out in unison, like a Greek chorus, "Hi, Tom!" Each person attending gave a personal progress report on the battle with addiction.

Posters with quaint slogans — "One day at a time," "You can do it" — decorated the dingy walls of the room. My friend believes such archaisms reveal another similarity to the early church. Most of the received wisdom of AA is passed down in oral traditions that date back to its founding more than fifty years before. Nobody much uses AA's up-to-date brochures and public relations pieces. Instead, they mainly rely on a fusty old book with the prosaic title *The Big Blue Book of Alcoholics Anonymous*, which tells the stories of the early members' lives in stilted, almost King Jamesian prose.

AA owns no property, has no headquarters with a massive direct mail facility and media center, no staff of well-paid consultants and investment counselors who jet across the country. The original founders of AA built in safeguards that would kill off anything that might lead to a bureaucracy. They believed their program could work only if it stayed at the most basic, intimate level: one alcoholic giving his or her life to help another. Yet AA has proven so effective that 250 other organizations, from Chocolaholics Anonymous to cancer patient groups, have sprung up in conscious mimicry of its technique.

The many parallels to the early church are no mere

historical accident. The Christian founders insisted that dependence on God be a mandatory part of the program. The night I attended, everyone in the room repeated aloud the twelve principles, which acknowledge total dependence on God for forgiveness and strength. (More agnostic members may substitute the euphemism "Higher Power," but after awhile that begins to seem inane and they usually revert to "God.") In the sharing time, some of the people would use God's name in a string of profanity, and in the very next sentence thank him for helping them make it through another week.

My friend freely admits that AA has replaced the church for him, and this fact sometimes troubles him. He calls it "the Christological question" of AA. "It has no theology to speak of. You rarely hear about Christ. AA groups borrow the sociology of the church, along with a few of the words and concepts, but they have no underlying doctrine. I miss that, but mainly I'm trying to survive, and AA helps me in that struggle far better than any local church." The church — many steeples loom within sight of the building where AA meets — seems irrelevant, vapid, and gutless to him. Others in the group explain their resistance by recounting stories of rejection, judgment, "a guilt trip." A local church is the last place they would stand up and declare, "Hi, I'm Tom. I'm an alcoholic and a drug addict." No one would holler back, "Hi, Tom!"

My friend thinks he will find himself back in the arms of the church someday, and he has not abandoned the faith. In fact, he says, involvement in AA has helped him resolve some of Christianity's most difficult paradoxes. Take the free will/determinism debate: how can a person accept full responsibility for her actions even when she knows that family background, hormonal imbalances, and supernatural forces of evil all contribute to that behavior? One of William Faulkner's characters put it this way, "I ain't got to. But I can't help it." AA is far less equivocal: every alcoholic has to acknowledge full and complete responsibility for *all* behavior, even what happens during a drunken stupor or "blackout" (a limbo state in which an alcoholic continues to function, but amnesically, with no conscious awareness). Rationalizations are forbidden.

"AA has helped me accept the notion of original sin too," my friend continues. "In fact, although many Christians balk at the doctrine, original sin makes perfect sense to the average AA person. We express that truth every time we introduce ourselves: 'I'm Tom. I'm an alcoholic.' No one ever gets away with saying, 'I *was* an alcoholic.' "

For my friend, immersion into Alcoholics Anonymous has meant salvation in the most literal sense. He knows that one slip could — no, will — send him to an early death. More than once, his AA partner has responded to his calls at four a.m., only to find him slouched in the eerie brightness of an all-night restaurant where he is filling a notebook, like a punished schoolchild, with the single sentence, "God help me make it through the next five minutes." Now he is approaching the five-year anniversary of sobriety — an important milestone by AA reckoning. And yet he knows that fifty percent of those who reach that milestone eventually fall away.

I came away from the "midnight church" impressed, but also wondering why AA meets needs in a way that the local church does not — or at least did not, for my friend. I asked him to name the one quality missing in the local church that AA had somehow provided. He stared at his cup of coffee for a long time, watching it go cold. I expected to hear a word like love or acceptance or, knowing him, perhaps anti-institutionalism. Instead, he said softly this one word: dependency.

"None of us can make it on our own — isn't that why Jesus came?" he explained. "Yet most church people give off a self-satisfied air of piety or superiority. I don't sense them consciously leaning on God or each other. Their lives appear to be in order. An alcoholic who goes to church feels inferior and incomplete." He sat in silence for a while, until a smile began to crease his face. "It's a funny thing," he said at last. "What I hate most about myself, my alcoholism, was the one thing God used to bring me back to him. Because of it, I know I can't survive without him. Maybe that's the redeeming value of alcoholics. Maybe God is calling us alcoholics to teach the saints what it means to be dependent on him and on his community on earth."

Jogging Past the AIDS Clinic

Some of my best "reading" time occurs as I jog along Chicago's lakefront, outfitted with Walkman and headphones, listening to books recorded on cassette tape. One winter the city's dingy streets and rat-gray skies formed a perfect backdrop for the book I had selected: Daniel Defoe's *A Journal of the Plague Year*. In meticulous, matter-of-fact prose he describes the bubonic plague that afflicted London in 1665.

In the account (which renders history in the form of realistic fiction), Defoe wanders the streets of a ghost city. Over 200,000 people have fled London, and those who remain barricade themselves indoors, terrified of human contact. On main thoroughfares, where steady streams of people once trod, new grass grows. "Sorrow and sadness

46

sat upon every face," says Defoe. At the peak of the plague, 1500 to 1700 people died each day, their bodies collected nightly for burial in cavernous open pits. The book describes gruesome scenes: dead children locked in the permanent grip of their parents' rigor mortis, live babies sucking in vain at the breasts of just-dead mothers.

As I listened, Defoe's account took on particular poignancy in view of a modern-day plague. My wife and I live in a neighborhood populated by many gays and not a few drug users. I could not avoid reflecting on the parallels between Defoe's time and our own as I jogged past a clinic for AIDS patients and dodged lampposts plastered with "AIDS Benefit" posters. Compared with the Great Plague, the AIDS epidemic has afflicted a much smaller proportion of the population, but it has stirred up a remarkably similar response of hysteria.

In Defoe's day, it seemed that God's molten wrath was being poured out on the entire planet. Two bright comets appeared in the sky each night — sure signs, said some, of God's hand behind the plague. Wild-eyed prophets roamed the streets, one echoing Jonah with his cry, "Yet forty days and London shall be destroyed!" Another walked around naked, balancing a pan of burning charcoal on his head to symbolize God's judgment. Still another naked prophet dolefully repeated the same phrase all day long: "Oh, the great and dreadful God! Oh, the great and dreadful God. . . ."

We have our modern version of these prophets. Most are well clothed, however, and they tend to narrow the focal point of God's judgment down to one particular group, the homosexuals, who are disproportionately represented among AIDS sufferers in the U.S. In some circles

I can almost detect a sigh of relief, a satisfaction that at last "they are getting what they deserve." Former Surgeon General C. Everett Koop, an evangelical Christian, received boxes full of hate mail whenever he dared to suggest otherwise.

The AIDS crisis taps into a mysterious yearning among human beings, a deep-rooted desire that suffering ought to be tied to behavior. I have a book on my shelf, *Theories of Illness*, that surveys 139 tribal groups from around the world; all but four of them perceive illness as a sign of God's (or the gods') disapproval. The author notes that the few who doubt such doctrine probably changed their beliefs after prolonged contact with modern civilization.

Virtually alone among all civilizations in history, our modern, secular one questions whether God plays a direct role in such human events as plagues and natural catastrophes. (Even we have our doubts: insurance policies specify certain "acts of God.") We are confused. Did God single out one town in the Southeast to be leveled by a tornado, as a message of judgment? Does he withhold rains from Africa as a sign of his displeasure? No one knows for sure. But AIDS — ah, there's a different story. Beyond dispute, the likelihood of AIDS transmission increases among those who engage in promiscuous sex, or share dirty needles.

For some Christians, AIDS seems to satisfy at last the longing for a precise connection between behavior and suffering-as-punishment. In a general sense, the connection has been established — in the same way that smoking increases risk of cancer, obesity increases risk of heart disease, and heterosexual promiscuity increases risk of venereal disease. The natural consequences of such behavior include, in many cases, physical suffering; scientists recognize this fact and advertise it widely. But the lurking question remains: Did God send AIDS as a specific, targeted punishment?

Other Christians are not so sure. They see a grave danger in playing God, or even interpreting history on his behalf. Like Job's friends, we can too easily come across as cranky or smug, not prophetic. "Vengeance is mine," God said, and whenever we mortals try to appropriate his vengeance, we tread on dangerous ground. Judgment without love makes enemies, not converts. Among the gays in my neighborhood, Christians' statements about the AIDS crisis have done little to encourage reconciliation.

Even the apparent cause-and-effect tie to behavior in AIDS raises troubling questions. What of "innocent" sufferers, such as the babies born to infected mothers or those who received the virus in a blood transfusion? Are they tokens of God's judgment? And if a cure is suddenly found — will that signify an end to God's punishment? Theologians in Europe expostulated for *four centuries* about God's message in The Great Plague; but it took only a little rat poison to silence all those anguished questions.

Reflecting on these two plagues, the scourge of the buboes that killed off a third of humanity and the modern scourge with its kindred hysteria, I find myself turning to an incident from Jesus' life recorded in Luke 13:1-5. When some people asked him about a contemporary tragedy, here is how he responded:

> Do you think that these Galileans were worse sinners than all the other Galileans because they suffered this way? I

tell you, no! But unless you repent, you too will all perish. Or those eighteen who died when the tower in Siloam fell on them — do you think they were more guilty than all the others living in Jerusalem? I tell you, no! But unless you repent, you too will all perish.

Then Jesus followed up with a parable about God's restraining mercy. He seems to imply that we "bystanders" of catastrophe have as much to learn from the event as do the sufferers themselves. What should a plague teach us? Humility, for one thing. And gratitude that God has so far withheld the judgment all of us deserve. And compassion, the compassion that Jesus displayed to all who mourn and suffer. Finally, catastrophe joins together victim and bystander in a common call to repentance, by abruptly reminding us of the brevity of life. It warns us to make ourselves ready in case we are the next victim of a falling tower — or an AIDS virus.

I have yet to find any support in the Bible for an attitude of smugness: *Ah, they deserve their punishment; watch them squirm.* Indeed, the message of a plague seems directed to survivors as much as to the afflicted. I guess AIDS holds as much meaning for those of us who jog past the clinics as for those who suffer inside.

Not a Bad Place to Start

Visitors to India sometimes claim they could recognize the country by its odor, even if led off a plane blindfolded. To my Western nose, it seems to comprise relatively equal parts of incense/stale urine/sandalwood/cow dung/flowers/diesel fumes/dust/camphor tree. Blend together molecules from all those and you will, I suspect, have something of the redolence of India. When I visited, I accompanied a true lover of India, Dr. Paul Brand, who had spent nearly half his life there. He led me on an unforgettable tour of Indian medical work.

In some respects, medicine in India differs little from that in the U.S. and Europe; the doctors are, after all, often trained at the same schools. You can find CAT scanners, magnetic resonance imagers, and other products of technological wizardry scattered across the subcontinent. But out beyond the cities, in India's million villages, medicine can be downright adventuresome. How does an Indian doctor rehydrate cholera victims when no sterile water is available? Why, he hangs a fresh coconut on the IV stand, of course: the glucose mixture in the airtight coconut is as sterile, and nearly as nutritious, as any product from a medical supply house. Still, it is a bit jarring to see a long rubber tube snaking up from a patient's arm to a shiny green coconut.

In the U.S. the Red Cross must constantly appeal for fresh blood. But in India, where donors are offered a small payment, new problems arise. A laborer can earn more money from a donation of blood than from a day's hard labor. How do you prevent an enterprising rickshaw driver, say, from going to a different hospital every few days to donate a pint? Medical personnel have devised a method of tattooing in order to keep eager donors from depleting their bodies' blood reserves.

Even the most modern hospitals, such as the Christian Medical College Hospital in Vellore, must cope with the ubiquitous problem of animal intruders. In Vellore, crows used to conspire together to steal patients' food. One of the canny birds would lead the assault, flying in an open door to tug at the tray cloth with its beak. When all the food spilled onto the floor, co-conspirators would swoop in for the feast. They had learned to ignore the gestures and yells of invalid patients. Eventually, the hospital crow-proofed its corridors with fine steel mesh; now Vellore is working on ways to keep the monkeys out.

The practice of medical missions in India is undergoing change. Western denominations and missions have cut back support in order to encourage mission hospitals to become more indigenous, but the well-intentioned policy may be backfiring. To survive, the hospitals must offer specialized, elite services that will attract paying clients. Thus many mission hospitals, no longer able to provide free services, must send the needy to government facilities or simply turn them away. The more progressive of these hospitals are searching for ways to overcome this problem, and CMC Hospital in Vellore is often looked up to as a model.

Vellore has had a reputation as being one of the very best medical institutions in Asia. Among India's hospitals, CMC was the first to offer thoracic surgery, kidney dialysis, open heart surgery, electron microscopy, and neurosurgery. It is not uncommon for Arabian princes to travel to the backwater town of Vellore for treatment. Some years ago, however, the directors at Vellore realized they were overtraining their students for village health care. A CMC-trained doctor could hardly make a diagnosis without access to an EKG machine and sophisticated chemical analyzers. To counteract this trend, the school erected a separate hospital, featuring open-air, mud-wall-and-thatch construction, to duplicate conditions at the village level. Now CMC students must supplement their training at that hospital, using only the medical resources common to India's remote villages.

In addition, CMC sponsors regular excursions to outlying villages. On a given day a month, every ill or injured person in a designated village gathers under a certain tamarind tree. A CMC van arrives, and the young doctors and assistants pile out, set up examining tables, and begin their routines of injections, bone-splints, and minor surgery. Thus the medical college training now encompasses three levels of care: sophisticated in-hospital services, a scaled-down rural hospital, and basic mobile clinics. Now not hundreds, but scores of thousands, of patients receive care each month.

The nation of India cannot hope to provide the most basic medical care to all her people. Only twenty percent of the population has sewer facilities and safe water. One need only visit the holy city of Varanasi, on the Ganges River, to see what the health professionals are up against. Carcasses of dogs and water buffaloes float by, sometimes used as rafts by the feeding vultures. Sacred cows wade at will into the water, defecating and urinating. And yet thousands of pilgrims each day come to the bathing ghats for their ritual baths: they dip seven times in the river, use it to brush their teeth, and then solemnly swallow the holy water.

It will take a virtual revolution just to change the local population's perceptions about health, let alone create the superstructure to offer them treatment. But there is hope, much of which comes in the name of Christ. One telling statistic reveals the fruit of two centuries of faithful mission work: of India's nearly one billion citizens, less than 3 percent call themselves Christian, and yet Christians are responsible for more than 18 percent of the nation's health care. A population half the size of the United States, comprising Hindus, Moslems, Sikhs, Jains, Parsis, and Communists, receives its medical care from people trained in places like Vellore.

Despite the many bumbling errors of paternalistic missionaries, the Christians have given India an inspired legacy of education and medicine. If you say the word

"Christian" to an Indian peasant — who may never have heard of Jesus Christ — the first image to pop into her mind may well be that of a hospital, or of a medical van that stops by her village once a month to provide free, personal care in Christ's name. It's certainly not the whole of the gospel, but it's not a bad place to start.

Morality That Pays

"A village of broad lawns and narrow minds," Ernest Hemingway once described his hometown of Oak Park, Illinois. But modern Oak Park is trying to reverse Hemingway's adjectives with a valiant attempt at broad-mindedness. Not long ago the woodsy Chicago suburb devised a cash merit system to reward citizens willing to try integrated housing.

It works like this: If you own an apartment building occupied by members of one race only, you can earn a $1000 bonus by letting the village help you select your renters. They will seek out minority families to move into all-white housing, and white families to move into all-black housing. The planners hope that such incentives will make it desirable for landlords to integrate their properties.

The law reminds me of a fair housing proposal play-fully suggested in *Harper's* magazine over a decade ago. "Let's face it," began the author, "appeals to morality and high ideals never convince Americans to change their behavior patterns. The only way to produce change is to make it financially worth our while. *Then* you'll see some action." The author went on to present a national program far more sweeping than Oak Park's. What would happen, he asked with tongue not quite in cheek, if Congress passed a law granting a $4000 annual tax deduction to any family who lived next door to a member of a minority race?

According to the author the federal treasury could actually save money by dismantling far less effective fair-housing programs. And overnight the free market would work miracles of racial reconciliation. Property values would rise, not fall, when a community integrated, thus making minorities the most sought-after residents. Advertisements like this would appear in local papers: "$1500 cash to any black or Hispanic family willing to move to the 700 block of Conwell Street. Will pay all moving expenses. Free prizes from local merchants!"

The cash-for-morality approach, first suggested in a whimsical article and now openly legislated in Oak Park, offers a quintessentially American solution to a social problem. It combines naive ingenuity with the old-fashioned profit motive. Will the most hardened bigot be able to resist a lucrative cash incentive?

*　　*　　*

Oak Park made the news again when former President Jimmy Carter made a fund-raising appearance there on behalf of a Christian organization called Habitat for Humanity. After the fancy banquet, he showed up in a rather squalid neighborhood in Chicago wearing blue jeans and a work shirt. Once again Carter was contributing his carpentry skills to help rebuild dilapidated inner-city houses. News cameramen could not seem to get enough footage of the former world leader wielding a hammer in the slums of Chicago.

Habitat for Humanity offers a different approach to social problems than that under experiment in Oak Park. The organization operates not in affluent suburbs but in rundown areas hidden away in aging cities, where no one wants to live. Participants don't receive cash bonuses; rather, volunteers like Jimmy Carter work long hours without pay. The poverty families selected to live in the rehabbed houses work alongside these volunteers, building up "sweat equity." No one realizes any investment gain or tax savings; Habitat grants no-interest loans to the new owners. In places like Chicago, committed Christian couples move into the neighborhood, offering role models for the poor and bringing social stability to the area.

These two approaches to the same problem got me thinking about the whole issue of social change. Both the Oak Park City Council and Habitat for Humanity share common goals: good, reasonable housing for the poor, and some way to break the discrimination deadlock. But their techniques for reaching those goals differ vastly. Oak Park hopes to "fix" its society by changing first the environments and ultimately the value systems of various minority groups. To accomplish that goal, they rely on a powerful motivator: human greed. Their plan is creative and rational — an example of the kingdom of this world at its best.

Habitat for Humanity, in contrast, is working to produce a far more radical change among a smaller group of people. They believe it is not enough for people with resources to invite in well-screened representatives of minority groups. Rather, people of resources must go, voluntarily, to the places of need, and give their time, and their sweat, and their families, and their love. They hope to change not merely the human environment, but the human heart. Not even the powerful motivator of greed is strong enough to accomplish that task. Their plan involves both risk and sacrifice, with no guarantee of reward — the kingdom that is not of this world, at its best.

Chicagoans saw two different news clips of Jimmy Carter: the distinguished former President speaking at a dress-up affair in Oak Park and then the same man swinging a hammer on the West Side of Chicago. Mr. Carter has had his feet in both kingdoms. At one time he could have ordered up housing for thousands with a stroke of his pen. Now he helps out the poor just like anybody else: in person, one nail at a time. As I watched the juxtaposition of the news reports of Carter's visit, I could not help wondering which approach gave him more personal satisfaction.

One thing troubled me, though: why is it that when a former President comes to town to build houses for the poor, hundreds of people will pay $50 to hear him talk about it at a fancy banquet, but only a handful will take up hammers and join him on the West Side?

Scorpions, Worms, and Missiles

Once I lay sleepless through a long night inside a tent in Somalia. The African refugee crisis — one of a series — was at its height then, and I was visiting a camp on a writing assignment. Tents and makeshift shelters stretched out for many acres around me, the huts squatting against the horizon in hummocky rows. They housed over 60,000 refugees. The night was warm, and I wanted to walk through the camp staring upward, for the Milky Way shone spectacularly in the clear equatorial sky. But camp workers had warned against nighttime strolls, because of the scorpions.

They told horrific stories of scorpions that lurked maliciously in towels and clothing, especially shoes. Victims of their bites must endure a pain like no other —

"childbirth times twelve," said one nurse — for at least two weeks. Just recently, a small scorpion had dropped from the slope of a tent onto the face of a sleeping doctor; he was still getting Novocain injections in his cheek, one every four hours, in an attempt to quell the pain.

As I lay awake I could hear a faint, eerie sound, somewhat like the keening death wail of a Moslem woman, though in tone more animal than human. This, I learned, was the sound of a Somali nomad who had been bitten by a scorpion. It carried far through the thin desert air, increasing in volume with each passing hour. At daybreak the nomad reached the refugee camp for treatment.

I left the camp after a few days, and as my truck pulled away from the camp, a chilling realization set in. The camp doctor had told me that one in six refugees would likely die of malnutrition or disease within the next month. But it struck me with awful force that during my stay in the camp I had spent far more energy and time worrying about those damnable scorpions than about the 10,000 refugees destined to die.

*   *   *

Once a Hebrew prophet named Jonah sat under the shade of a vine just outside the great city of Nineveh. When a worm chewed through the vine, exposing Jonah to the blazing sun and a scorching east wind, he became sullen, bitter, and angry enough to die.

God chose that particular moment to give Jonah a lesson in divine priorities. Even after the episode with the great fish, Jonah had never fully accepted his assignment

as missionary to the Assyrians. *Assyrians!* The veritable
Nazis of their day. This cruel, godless people, who razed
whole civilizations and led captives away with hooks in
their mouths, hardly deserved another chance. It was the
height of insult to send him, a Hebrew prophet, to his
archenemies. Who cared if Nineveh got destroyed in forty
days; the more brimstone, the better.

But this is what God said to the sulky prophet: "You
have been concerned about this vine, though you did not
tend it or make it grow. It sprang up overnight and died
overnight. But Nineveh has more than a hundred and
twenty thousand people who cannot tell their right hand
from their left, and many cattle as well. Should I not be
concerned about that great city?"

*   *   *

Once upon a time some officials high up in the United
States government sat around a table discussing ways to
free Americans being held hostage in the Middle East. Of
their various attempts, only one bore fruit, a plan that
involved the shipment of millions of dollars of military
hardware to Iran.

When the news broke, newspapers were filled with
stories about the arms-for-hostages swap. Editorials expressed outrage that the United States had bargained
with a hostile nation that sponsors terrorism. Congress-
men decried the fact that profits from the arms sale had
been siphoned off to support an embargoed war in Central America. Committee members and special investiga-
tors pored over shipping documents and logs of tele-
phone calls to determine who knew what, and when.

Were any laws violated? Had the White House upset the constitutional balance of power? These were the questions hotly debated each evening on the network news, and these the issues that seriously weakened the Reagan administration in its final two years.

Strangely, very few people voiced aloud what seems to me the most basic issue of all, the fundamental moral issue behind the bartering. Essentially, America was offering sixty million dollars' worth of weapons — devices brilliantly engineered to cause death — in order to save the hostages' lives. Looked at mathematically, we were trading the deaths of scores of Iraqis (the people on the receiving end of those missiles, who were our allies at the time) for the lives of six Americans. Oliver North actually tried to compute the mathematics involved. He noted in one memo to his boss John Poindexter: "1 707 w/300 TOWs = 1 AMCIT," which he later explained as meaning "One Boeing 707 loaded with 300 TOW anti-tank missiles equals one American citizen."

Shortly after one of the arms deliveries to Iran, an Iranian missile fell in the streets of Baghdad, Iraq, killing forty-eight civilians. Had that missile been obtained in the deal for hostages? In all, 2000 anti-tank missiles were shipped to Iran. What if only ten percent of those missiles found their mark, hitting 200 Iraqi tanks and killing two soldiers in each one? The arithmetic is obvious: 400 dead Iraqis in exchange for six (or three, as it turned out) live Americans.

I do not question our nation's right to defend its citizens by force. But perhaps we missed a lesson in all the fuss, and miss it still as we blithely ship billions of dollars of weapons overseas each year. And perhaps my experience in Somalia and Jonah's in Assyria, so radically different from the circumstances surrounding "Irangate," point to the same underlying moral issue.

Is my own physical comfort more significant than the survival of 10,000 refugees? Is the comfort of one Hebrew prophet more important than the lives of 120,000 Assyrian children? And how many foreigners' deaths are worth six American lives?

It is a curious coincidence of geography that the ruins of the ancient Assyrian city of Nineveh lie within the borders of modern-day Iraq.

Pinochet and the Pope

By pure coincidence, I happened to be in Santiago, Chile, on a day when Pope John Paul II paid a visit. It was a sunny afternoon in April when I leaned out a hotel window there, craning my neck for a glimpse of the motorcade. A million other people were awaiting him too, in rows ten deep lining the streets of a city that had been scrubbed and painted and festooned with white-and-yellow papal banners. Army snipers patrolled the rooftops. A helicopter clattered noisily overhead.

When the Pope's motorized glass bubble — *papamobile*, the Chileans called it — rounded the corner, the street erupted in a burst of joy and a blizzard of confetti. Then suddenly, almost in mid-breath, the thunderous cheers turned to catcalls and whistles. The abrupt change

puzzled me until I saw, just behind the papamobile, a
squat, ugly armored car with a narrow slit window; inside
that vehicle rode General Augusto Pinochet, then president of Chile. I couldn't help wondering what was going
through Pinochet's mind: *What's the Pope's secret!? He
waves and the whole country goes into a swoon.* There was a
spirit loose in Santiago that must have baffled him.

The next night 80,000 Chilean teenagers filled a
stadium to hear the Pope speak. A dark cloud of memory
hung over the stadium, for in 1973 Pinochet had used it
as a holding pen for dissidents. Scores were killed then,
and hundreds tortured. (Church-sponsored human rights
groups estimate that 7000 Chileans were killed by government troops during Pinochet's regime.) Sometimes, as a
counterpoint to their adulation of the Pope, the teenagers
at the rally broke out in spontaneous chants: "Go away,
Pin-o-chet."

Earlier that day, 600,000 people had turned out to
see the pope at an outdoor "town meeting" in one of
Santiago's worst slums. "Love is stronger than hate," the
Pope kept saying to the crowds. But hate has its cham-
pions in Chile as well. The night of the stadium rally I
found myself swept up in a throng of demonstrating
students on Santiago's main boulevard. It began as a
simple holding-hands-we-shall-overcome type of march.
"John Paul, take the tyrant with you," the students
chanted. But when one of the crowd tossed a rock through
a shop window, the sharp, percussive sound seemed to
arouse a primordial mob instinct. Fires flared spon-
taneously in a dozen places, and the students began rip-
ping up iron grillwork along the boulevard's median
strip.

Soon a dilapidated bus appeared, filled with soldiers. It zigzagged toward the crowd, like a crazed lion plunging into a herd of wildebeests. The students scattered, then regrouped, then counter-attacked. I heard the ugly *thunk* of rocks hitting metal, and more sounds of glass breaking, and then the angry wail of a siren. The mood on the street seemed to be approaching a flashpoint until a huge vehicle shaped like a weird, ungainly insect arrived. It was the *guanaco* (named for a spitting llama), a water cannon, and the students knew it well. In what seemed like seconds they all melted into the darkness, and the boulevard was suddenly empty. I returned to my hotel and joined other guests gathered around a lobby television set, watching the Pope pray for peace.

*   *   *

International travel often brings unexpected ironies to light. A few days later I was in Lima, Peru, touring a rather somber historic building. A guidebook had directed me there, to view "one of the finest examples of baroque in South America." Sure enough, a large upstairs room disclosed wonderfully preserved tilework and an intricate mahogany ceiling. But, bizarrely, in the center of the room stood a cross, with a hand-carved head of Christ mounted on the top. I was standing in the notorious Court of the Inquisition, a room where for two-and-a-half centuries (1570 to 1820) the church tried accused heretics. The Inquisitors — dressed in costumes with an uncanny resemblance to Ku Klux Klan getups — would first hear testimony about the defendant from accusers, who wore masks to protect their anonymity. Then, after the "jury" of church officials had deliberated, the Chief Inquisitor would announce the verdict via the cross. The manipulation of certain levers would cause Jesus' head to bob up and down, signifying the defendant's innocence. But if the head moved from side to side, the victim was sent to a dungeonlike area underneath the courtroom.

Visitors can view *in situ* the various torture techniques employed; dioramas below ground re-create them with primitive realism. Dummy Inquisitors assiduously work over the dummy victims, twisting piano wires into flesh, pouring water into nostrils, disarticulating limbs on a stretching rack. And it was while I was examining these displays in Lima that it dawned on me where modern South American countries learned their torture methodology. They learned from the church.

The church, both Catholic and Protestant, has experimented with various forms of power over the centuries. The power of brute force, such as that wielded in Lima's Court of the Inquisition, imposed theological orthodoxy on a population for 250 years. It proved effective, but at great cost: the continent has not yet recovered from the assault on freedom and human dignity. Leaders of that same church now seek a higher kind of power. I had seen this most strikingly from my hotel balcony in Santiago: through sheer moral force the Pope commanded more of Chile's loyalty than did Pinochet with all his vaunted power. The prophet Isaiah alluded to such "higher" power in this reference to the Messiah:

> He will strike the earth with the rod of his mouth;
> with the breath of his lips he will slay the wicked.

The juxtaposition of two images — the Pope calling for love in Santiago, and the Inquisitors administering their truth-enforcers in Lima — brought to mind a passage from Scottish writer George MacDonald. Why is God so restrained in the face of the world's evil? wondered MacDonald. Why did Jesus Christ take such a passive role when threatened with violence? This is what MacDonald concluded:

> Instead of crushing the power of evil by divine force; instead of compelling justice and destroying the wicked; instead of making peace on the earth by the rule of a perfect prince; instead of gathering the children of Jerusalem under His wings whether they would or not, and saving them from the horrors that anguished His prophetic soul — He let evil work its will while it lived; He contented himself with the slow unencouraging ways of help essential; making men good; casting out, not merely controlling Satan. . . . Throughout His life on earth, He resisted every impulse to work more rapidly for a lower good — strong, perhaps, when He saw old age and innocence and righteousness trodden under foot.

MacDonald adds one sentence, a poignant reminder for all of us: "To love righteousness is to make it grow, not to avenge it."

Moral force, to be sure, is a risky form of power. When compared to the glaring reality of brute force, it may appear weak and ineffectual. But it has its own method of conquering. Perhaps if General Pinochet had understood the distinction between the two kinds of

power, he would know why the cheers in Santiago
changed to boos as his armored car approached.

A Haunting Deathbed Confession

Although Simon Wiesenthal himself survived the German concentration camps, he lost eighty-nine family members to the Nazis. Since then, he has devoted much of his life to tracking down former Nazis and war criminals. People often ask about his obsession: why hunt men in their seventies and eighties for crimes committed half a century ago? Is there no forgiveness for such people? No reconciliation? Wiesenthal set down his personal answers to such questions in a slim, powerful book called *The Sunflower.*

The book begins with a haunting story, a remembrance of an event that took place during Wiesenthal's imprisonment. He was selected at random from a work detail, yanked aside, and taken up a back stairway to a hospital corridor. A nurse led him into a darkened room, then left him alone with a pitiful figure wrapped in white, lying on a bed. It was a German officer, badly wounded, swathed in yellow-stained bandages. Gauze covered his entire face.

In a weakened, trembling voice, the officer proceeded to offer a kind of sacramental confession to Wiesenthal. He recounted his boyhood and early days in the Hitler Youth movement. He told of action along the Russian front, and of the increasingly harsh measures his SS unit had taken against the Jewish populace. And then he told of a terrible atrocity, when his unit herded all the Jews from one town into a wooden frame building and torched it. Some of the Jews, their clothes and hair ablaze, leaped in desperation from the second floor, and the SS soldiers — he among them — shot them as they fell. He started to tell of one child in particular, a young boy with black hair and dark eyes, but his voice gave way.

Several times Wiesenthal tried to leave the room, but each time the mummy-like figure would reach out with a cold, bloodless hand and constrain him. Finally, after maybe two hours, the officer explained why he had summoned a Jewish prisoner. He had asked a nurse whether any Jews still existed; if so, he wanted one brought to his room for a last rite before death. "I know that what I am asking is almost too much for you," he said. "But without your answer I cannot die in peace." And then he asked for forgiveness for all his crimes against the Jews. He was imploring a prisoner who the next day might die at the hands of SS comrades.

Wiesenthal stood in silence for some time, staring at the man's bandaged face. At last he made up his mind and left the room, without saying a word. He left the soldier in torment, unforgiven.

Wiesenthal's book devotes ninety pages to that story. For the next 105 pages, he lets others speak. He sent the story to thirty-two thinkers — Jewish rabbis, Christian theologians, secular philosophers and ethicists — and asked for their responses. Had he done right? Should he have forgiven the dying SS criminal? The vast majority of respondents replied that Wiesenthal was right in leaving the soldier unforgiven. Only six thought he had done wrong.

Some of the non-Christian respondents questioned the whole idea of forgiveness; they deemed it an irrational concept that merely lets criminals off the hook and perpetuates injustice. Others granted a place for forgiveness but considered the heinous crimes of the Nazis as beyond forgiveness. The most persuasive arguments came from those who insisted that forgiveness can be granted only by the people who have been wronged. What moral right, they asked, had Wiesenthal to grant forgiveness on behalf of the Jews who had died at this man's hand?

I am not prepared to pass judgment on the almost unbearable dilemma that confronted Simon Wiesenthal in the hospital room. At the least, the thirty-two responses prove his question has no easy resolution. But the Bible does add an interesting twist to one aspect of the dilemma he faced. It relates to an old-fashioned theological word that kept cropping up in Wiesenthal's book: "reconciliation." A phrase from the book of 2 Corinthians convinces me that we do have the right to offer forgiveness on behalf of another. In that passage, Paul announces that we have been given "the ministry of reconciliation." "We are therefore Christ's ambassadors," he continues, "as though God were making his appeal through us. We implore you on Christ's behalf: Be reconciled to God" (5:20). Paul bases the "ministry of reconciliation" on the example of Jesus, who voluntarily took on our sin so that we could, through him, attain the righteousness of God.

What does it mean to be a minister of reconciliation, an ambassador of Christ who proclaims forgiveness to those who did not sin against you personally? Some Christians are trying to put reconciliation into practice by going as "Witnesses for Peace" to hot spots in Central America and the Middle East, deliberately putting their bodies in the line of fire. Bishop Desmond Tutu led a government-sanctioned "Truth and Reconciliation Commission" in South Africa to help bring healing to that divided country. In the U.S., Chuck Colson's Prison Fellowship volunteers enter crowded, fear-filled cell blocks to proclaim forgiveness and love to people society has cast aside as guilty and unworthy.

Some churches have organized their outreach programs into a Ministry of Evangelism and a Ministry of Social Concerns. Should we consider a Ministry of Reconciliation? The needs are not only in Central America and Ireland. Wherever a marriage is breaking up, wherever a child has become estranged, wherever enmity separates races or social groups, a need for reconciliation exists: a need for someone to take on the burdens of others and to offer forgiveness even before it is sought.

One man, Will Campbell, has taken that phrase, "Be ye reconciled," as his life motto. In the autobiographical *Brother to a Dragonfly* he explains that his love and compassion once extended to Southern blacks and the oppressed, but not to rednecks and KKK members. After three close friends were murdered by the KKK, however, he heard a message from God that defied every human instinct. He was to go, as a minister of reconciliation, to the very group who had killed his friends. He was to become, and in fact did become, an "apostle to the rednecks."

I think the title "minister of reconciliation" was one Paul eagerly claimed for himself. He had reason. He, too, had a record of "war crimes," committed, in his case, against Christians. God forgave him for those crimes, and the apostle to the Gentiles never seemed to get over that startling feeling of being reconciled.

Merely Human

I used to meet with a gentle and wise pastor on a semi-regular basis. Often our time together was low-key and uneventful, but one afternoon will always remain seared in my memory. It was a blustery Chicago day, and I sat hunched in a wool sweater next to a hissing radiator. That day, I asked the questions. I had just read in a church newsletter article that the pastor, while serving in the Army in World War II, had participated in the liberation of the Dachau concentration camp. I asked him about the experience.

The pastor looked away from me to his right, seeming to focus on a blank space on the wall. He was silent for at least a minute. His eyes moved back and forth rapidly, as if working to fill in the scene from forty years before. Finally he spoke, and for the next twenty minutes he recalled the sights, the sounds, and the smells — especially the smells — that greeted his unit as they marched through the gates of Dachau just outside Munich. For weeks the soldiers had heard wild rumors about the camps, but, inured to war propaganda, they gave little credence to such talk. Nothing prepared them, and nothing could possibly prepare them, for what they found inside.

"A buddy and I were assigned to one boxcar. Inside were human corpses, stacked in neat rows, exactly like firewood. The Germans, ever meticulous, had planned out the rows — alternating the heads and feet, and accommodating different sizes and shapes of bodies. Our job was like moving furniture. We would pick up each body — so light! — and carry it to a designated area. Some fellows couldn't do this part. They stood by the barbed wire fences, retching.

"I couldn't believe it the first time we came across a person in the pile still alive. But it was true. Incredibly, some of the corpses weren't corpses. They were human beings. We yelled for doctors, and they went to work on these survivors right away.

"I spent two hours in the boxcar, two hours that for me included every known emotion: rage, pity, shame, revulsion — every negative emotion, I should say. They came in waves, all but the rage. It stayed, fueling our work. We had no other emotional vocabulary for such a scene.

"After we had taken the few survivors to a makeshift clinic, we turned our attention to the SS officers in charge of Dachau, who were being held under guard in a bunkhouse. Army Intelligence had set up an interrogation center nearby. It was outside the camp, and to reach it you had to walk down a ravine and through a copse of trees. The captain asked for a volunteer to escort a group of twelve SS prisoners to the interrogation center, and Chuck's hand shot right up.

"Chuck was the loudest, brashest, most volatile soldier in our company. He stood about five feet, four inches tall, but had overly long arms so that his hands hung down around his knees, like a gorilla's. He came from Cicero, a suburb of Chicago known mainly for its racism and its association with Al Capone. Chuck claimed to have worked for Capone before the war, and not one of us doubted it.

"Well, Chuck grabbed a submachine gun and prodded the group of SS prisoners down the trail. They walked ahead of him with their hands locked back behind their heads, their elbows sticking out on either side. A few minutes after they disappeared into the trees, we heard the rattly burp of a machine gun in three long bursts of fire. We all ducked; it could have been a German sniper in the woods. But soon Chuck came strolling out, smoke still curling from the tip of his weapon. 'They all tried to run away,' he said with a kind of leer."

I interrupted the story to ask if anyone reported what Chuck did or took disciplinary action. The pastor laughed and gave me a get-serious-this-is-war look.

"No, and that's what got to me. It was on that day that I felt called by God to become a pastor. First, there was the horror of the corpses in the boxcar. I could not absorb such a scene. I did not even know such Absolute Evil existed. But when I saw it, I knew beyond doubt that

I must spend my life serving whatever opposed such Evil — serving God.

"Then came the incident with Chuck. I had a nauseating fear that the captain might call on me to escort the next group of SS guards, and an even greater dread fear that if he did, I might do the same as Chuck. The beast that was within those guards was also within me."

*   *   *

I could not coax more reminiscing from the pastor that day. Either he had probed the past enough, or he felt obligated to move to our own agenda. But before we left the subject entirely, I asked a question that, as I look back now, seems almost impudent. "Tell me, after such a cosmic kind of call to ministry — confronting the great Evil of the century — how does it feel to fulfill that call by sitting in this office listening to middle-class Yuppies ramble on about their personal problems?"

His answer came back quickly, as if he had asked himself that question many times. "I do see a connection. Without being melodramatic, I sometimes wonder what might have happened if a skilled, sensitive person had befriended the young, impressionable Adolf Hitler as he wandered the streets of Vienna in his confused state. The world might have been spared all that bloodshed — spared Dachau. I never know who might be sitting in that chair you're occupying right now.

"And even if I end up spending my life with 'nobodies' . . . I learned in the boxcar that there's no such thing. Those corpses with a pulse were as close to no-bodies as you can get: mere skeletons wrapped in papery skin. But I would have done anything to keep those poor, ragged people alive. Our medics stayed up all night to save them; some in our company lost their lives to liberate them. There are no 'nobodies.' I learned that day in Dachau what 'the image of God' in a human being is all about."

Part III

Among the Believers

Should we be happy or sad about the resurgence of evangelical Christianity in America? Should America be happy or sad?

Should the world be able to tell if a person is a Christian just by looking? What does a Christian look like? What should a Christian look like? More like Mother Teresa or Madonna? Why do we prefer reading about people we don't really want to be like?

Why does the Bible rant about idolatry? What makes that quaint custom so offensive? Are there any idolaters in Peoria, Illinois?

Are there any Mormons in Peoria, Illinois? Do Mormons look any different from Christians? Should they?

Why do so few Christians exhibit joy? Would a joyful person look more like Mother Teresa or Madonna?

Why do modern authors, like John Updike, and modern TV shows, like "Baywatch," seem obsessed with human sexuality while the topic is barely mentioned in church, except as a warning?

Why do many Christians feel more guilty than forgiven? What does feeling forgiven feel like? If the gospel consists of grace, acceptance, and forgiveness, why do counselors see so many Christian clients riddled with guilt, self-hatred, and a spirit of criticism?

Love and Power

In the book *In Season, Out of Season,* Jacques Ellul, the now-deceased French sociologist, reflected on his long, productive life. Looking back, he saw that his thinking and actions proceeded along two parallel tracks. On a more activist, secular track he did pioneering work in the French Resistance, in city government, and in environmental causes. On another, spiritual track Ellul's Christian faith found expression in his devotional life and in his service as a pastor and seminary professor. Yet, with a tone of disillusionment, he admitted that he never successfully brought together the two tracks.

Ellul's disillusionment developed in the corridors of power, during his terms as a denominational leader and a politician. His experiences there caused him to question

whether change would ever come from within institutions. Can any structure convey Christian love and compassion? Ellul asked. Reading of his struggle started me
thinking about the wide crevasse that separates power
from love.

If we could chart the history of the Christian church
in a graph as simple and revealing as a stock market
report, we would see tremendous surges in the church's
power. First the Christian faith conquered the Near East,
and then Rome, then all of Europe. Finally it spread to
the New World and ultimately to Africa and Asia. Yet,
strangely enough, the peaks of success and earthly power
also mark the peaks of intolerance and religious cruelty,
those stains in church history we are most ashamed of
today. The conquistadors who converted the New World
at the point of a sword, the Christian explorers in Africa
who cooperated with the slave trade — we are still feeling
the aftershocks from their mistakes.

Throughout Christian history, love has had an un-
easy coexistence with power. For this reason, I worry
about the surge of power in the evangelical movement.
Once we were ignored or scorned. Now evangelicals are
often mentioned in the news and are courted by every
savvy politician — at least every savvy *Republican* politician. Various political movements have sprung up with
a distinctly evangelical scent to them. I find this trend at
once heartening and alarming. Why alarming? Regardless of the merits of a given issue — whether a prolife
lobby out of the Right or environmental lobby out of the
Left — political movements risk pulling onto themselves
the cloak of power that smothers love. A movement by
nature draws lines, makes distinctions, delivers judg-

ment; in contrast, love erases lines, overcomes distinctions, and dispenses grace.

Most assuredly, I am not calling for an ostrich-like stance of hiding from the issues that confront Christians in a secular society. They must be faced, and addressed, and legislated. But Paul's words continue to haunt me: If I speak in the tongues of men and of angels, and have the gift of prophecy and can fathom all mysteries and all knowledge, but have not love, I am nothing. Somehow — unless our power is to corrode like that of the well-intentioned religious leaders who preceded us — we must approach power with humility, and fear, and a consuming love for those we will exercise it over.

Jesus did not say, "All men will know you are my disciples . . . if you just pass laws, quash immorality, and restore decency to family and government," but rather ". . . if you love one another" (John 13:35). He made that statement, of course, the night before his death. Never have the contrasting styles of God's power and human power been more openly displayed. Human power, represented by the might of the Roman empire and the full force of Jewish religious authorities, collided head-on with God's power. Amazingly, at that moment God chose the path of deliberate powerlessness. He could have called on 10,000 angels, but did not. As I look back on that dark night, and also on other dark nights in history, I marvel at the restraint God has shown.

I believe God restrains himself for one reason: he knows the inherent limitation of any form of power. It can do everything but the most important thing. It cannot force love. In a concentration camp, as so many have borne poignant witness, the guards have ultimate power and can force anything. They can make you renounce your God, curse your family, work without pay, eat human excrement, kill and then bury your closest friend or even your own son. All this is within their power. Only one thing is not: love. They cannot force you to love them.

Love does not operate according to the rules of power, and it can never be forced. In that fact we can glimpse the thread of reason behind God's use (or non-use) of power. He is interested in only one thing from us: our love. That is why he created us. And no pyrotechnic displays of omnipotence will achieve that, only his ultimate emptying to join us and then die for us. Herein is love.

Every Sunday school child can quote the deepest theology: "God so loved the world that he gave his only Son." And, when it all boils down, that is what the Christian gospel is — not a demonstration of power, but a demonstration of love.

The Way Up

"Adam is a 25-year-old man who cannot speak, cannot dress or undress himself, cannot walk alone, cannot eat without much help. He does not cry or laugh. Only occasionally does he make eye contact. His back is distorted. His arm and leg movements are twisted. He suffers from severe epilepsy and, despite heavy medication, sees few days without grand-mal seizures. Sometimes, as he grows suddenly rigid, he utters a howling groan. On a few occasions I've seen one big tear roll down his cheek.

"It takes me about an hour and a half to wake Adam up, give him his medication, carry him into his bath, wash him, shave him, clean his teeth, dress him, walk him to the kitchen, give him his breakfast, put him in his wheel-

chair, and bring him to the place where he spends most
of the day with therapeutic exercises."

At the height of his career, author Henri Nouwen
moved from his post at Harvard University to a community called Daybreak, near Toronto, to take on the daily,
mundane chores related above. He ministered not to in-
tellectuals but to a young man who is considered by many
a vegetable, a useless person who should not have been
born. Yet up to the time of his death Nouwen insisted that
he, not Adam, was the chief beneficiary in this strange,
mis-fitted relationship.

From the hours spent with Adam, Nouwen said, he
gained an inner peace so fulfilling that it made most of
his other, more high-minded tasks seem boring and su-
perficial by contrast. Early on, as he sat beside that silent,
slow-breathing child-man, he realized how violent and
marked with rivalry and competition, how obsessive, was
his prior drive toward success in academia and Christian
ministry. From Adam he learned that "what makes us
human is not our mind but our heart, not our ability to
think but our ability to love. Whoever speaks about Adam
as a vegetable or animal-like creature misses the sacred
mystery that Adam is fully capable of receiving and
giving love." From Adam, Henri Nouwen learned —
gradually, painfully, shamefully — that the way up is
down.

*   *   *

My career as a journalist has afforded me opportunities
to interview diverse people. Looking back, I can roughly
divide them into two types: stars and servants. The stars

include NFL football greats, movie actors, music per-
formers, famous authors, TV personalities, and the like.
These are the people who dominate our magazines and
our television programs. We fawn over them, poring over
the minutiae of their lives: the clothes they wear, the food
they eat, the aerobic routines they follow, the people they
love, the toothpaste they use.

Yet I must tell you that, in my limited experience,
these our "idols" are as miserable a group of people as I
have ever met. Most have troubled or broken marriages.
Nearly all are hopelessly dependent on psychotherapy.
In a heavy irony, these larger-than-life heroes seem tor-
mented by incurable self-doubt.

I have also spent time with servants. People like Dr.
Paul Brand, who worked for twenty years among outcasts
— the poorest of the poor, leprosy patients in rural India.
Or the health workers who left high-paying jobs to serve
with Mendenhall Ministries in a backwater town of Mis-
sissippi. Or relief workers in Somalia, Sudan, Ethiopia,
Bangladesh, or other such repositories of world-class
human suffering. Or the Ph.D.'s scattered throughout
jungles of South America translating the Bible into obscure languages.

I was prepared to honor and admire these servants,
to hold them up as inspiring examples. I was not, however, prepared to envy them. But as I now reflect on the
two groups side by side, stars and servants, the servants
clearly emerge as the favored ones, the graced ones. They
work for low pay, long hours, and no applause, "wasting"
their talents and skills among the poor and uneducated.
But somehow in the process of losing their lives they have
found them. They have received the "peace that is not of

this world" such as Henri Nouwen described, a peace he discovered not within the stately quadrangles of Harvard, but by the bedside of incontinent Adam.

* * *

Along with many other Christians, I wince at the snidely jubilant tone that often characterizes media coverage of scandals among Christians. *See, those Christians are no better — no, they're worse — than the rest of us.* I grieve over reports that contributions to almost all Christian organizations decline dramatically in the wake of each new scandal. I consider my gifts to organizations like World Vision, American Leprosy Mission, World Concern, Wycliffe, and Mendenhall Ministries as the highest-returning investment I can possibly make.

Maybe one problem underlying the scandals of Christian superstars is that we distort the kingdom of God by training our spotlight not on the servants, but on the stars. As Henri Nouwen said, "Keep your eyes on the one who refuses to turn stones into bread, jump from great heights or rule with great temporal power. Keep your eyes on the one who says, 'Blessed are the poor, the gentle, those who mourn and those who hunger and thirst for righteousness; blessed are the merciful, the peacemakers and those who are persecuted in the cause of uprightness.' . . . Keep your eyes on the one who is poor with the poor, weak with the weak and rejected with the rejected. That one is the source of all peace." In other words, keep your eyes on the servant, not the star.

The Gospels repeat one saying of Jesus more than

any other: "Whoever wants to save his life will lose it, but whoever loses his life for my sake will find it." Truly, the way up is down.

Trivial Pursuits

You can hardly read the Bible without encountering the subject of idolatry: it ranks as by far the most common topic discussed. For us modern readers, though, a nagging question hangs over those passages: Why all the fuss? What's the big attraction with idols anyway? Why did the Hebrews, for example, keep deserting Yahweh, the God who had delivered them from Egypt, for the sake of carved tree trunks and bronze statues?

I gained insight into this issue on a visit to India, where idol worship flourishes. The four-star attractions in most Indian cities are temples erected to honor any of a thousand gods: monkey gods, elephant gods, erotic goddesses, snake gods, even a smallpox goddess. There,

I observed that idolatry tends to produce two contradictory results: magic and triviality.

For the devout, idolatry adds a dimension of magic to life. Hindus believe the gods control all events, including such natural disasters as monsoons, earthquakes, diseases, and traffic accidents. These powerful forces must be kept happy at all costs. But what pleases a god depends on the god's character, and Hindu gods can be fearsome and violent. Calcutta, India's largest city, has adopted the murderous goddess Kali, who is usually depicted wearing a garland of bloody heads around her waist. Devotion to such gods can easily lead to a paralyzing fear and virtual slavery to the gods' whims.

Other Hindus, less devout, take a different approach. They treat their gods as trivialities, almost like good-luck charms. A taxi driver mounts a tiny statue of a monkey god, draped with flowers, on the dashboard of his car. If you inquire, he'll say he prays to the god for safety — but you know about the traffic in India, he adds with a laugh.

Both these modern responses to idolatry illustrate what so alarmed the prophets of Israel. On the one hand, the taxi driver shows how idolatry can trivialize deity. Maybe the god will help you out, maybe not, but why not play along? Some Israelites adopted that spirit, drifting carelessly from god to god. No attitude could be further from that demanded by Yahweh, the true God. He had chosen the Hebrews as a kingdom of priests, a peculiar people set apart. He mocked the ludicrousness of carving a god out of a tree, then using branches from the same tree to cook a meal (Isa. 44:16). He is Lord of the Universe, not a good-luck charm.

Far too often, however, idols in the Middle East took a more sinister form, more resembling the evil goddess of Calcutta. Followers worshiped Baal, for example, by having sex in the temple with prostitutes, or even by killing a human baby as a sacrifice. Such attitudes toward worship could not possibly coexist with devotion to Yahweh. The god Baal-Zebub, meaning "Lord of the flies," ultimately became a synonym for Satan himself (see Matt. 10:25).

Why did sinister idols like Baal prove so irresistible? Like farm kids gawking at big-city life, the Israelites moved from forty years of wilderness wanderings into a land of superior cultural achievement. When they settled down to the new occupation of farming, they looked to a Canaanite deity, Baal, for help in controlling the weather. In other words, they sought a shortcut through magic. Similarly, when a mighty army rose up to threaten their borders, the Hebrews borrowed a few of that army's favorite idols, hedging their bets in case their own religion failed to bring them military success. Idols became a phantom source of power, an alternative place to invest faith and hope.

The worship of graven images disappeared from Israel only after God took the extreme measure of dismantling the nation. But other, more subtle forms of idolatry persisted, and persist to this day. According to the New Testament, idolatry need not involve images of wood or stone. Anything that tempts us away from the true God may function as an idol.

In our modern society, dominated by appeals to image and status, idols abound. Not surprisingly, idolatry produces the same results in us today that it did in the

Israelites. Some gods — Mammon, beauty, success — appeal to our thirst for magic. On the human level, they work spectacularly, giving us a kind of magical power over other people's lives as well as our own. I worry more, however, about the false gods that escape easy detection, the ones that tend toward triviality, not magic. In classical idolatry, a visible symbol expressed the change of loyalty that had gone on inside. Most of our idols today are invisible, harder to detect.

What modern idols make God seem trivial? What tends to reduce the surprise, the passion, the vitality of my relationship with God? Most days, I am not so conscious of choosing between a god and God; the alternatives do not present themselves so clearly. Rather, I find God edged out by a series of small distractions. A car that needs repair, last-minute plans for an upcoming trip, a leaky gutter, a friend's wedding — these distractions, mere trivialities, may lead to a form of *forgetfulness* that resembles idolatry in its most dangerous form. The busyness of life, including all its religious busyness, can crowd out God. I confess that some days I meet people, work, make decisions, talk on the phone, all without giving God a single thought.

A friend of mine was stopped dead in her tracks by a skeptic. After listening to her explain her faith, he said this: "But you don't *act* like you believe God is alive." I try to turn his accusation into a question: Do I act like God is alive? It is a good question, one that lies at the heart of all idolatry, and one that I must ask myself again every day.

Mormons, Pharisees, and Other Good Folks

Some Mormons will tell you they converted on a visit to Salt Lake City, and understandably so. It's hard not to be impressed by the bustling downtown area. City streets are clean and well-maintained, and intersections come equipped with electronic chirpers to guide blind pedestrians. Everyone seems to live in a house from *Leave It to Beaver*, and Utah kids have such a fresh-scrubbed look they practically glow. You have to search far and wide to find a counter-culture, and this in a state separated from California only by the impiety of Nevada. Perhaps neuroses fester underneath, but externally the Utah society appears to work.

Some years ago, the Mormons spent millions of dollars in a series of self-congratulatory evangelism pamphlets. The first, which appeared as a twelve-page insert in *Reader's Digest*, described their healthy, upright style of life. For Mormons, home and family come first, the pamphlet said. "It will be a family likely to be admired by neighbors for its quiet competence and self-assurance, and generally envied for its closeness and good-natured round of shared activities. . . . Think of the Osmond family, George, Olive, their eight sons, and Marie: clean, bright, outgoing, bringing music to millions and loving it." Mormons try to practice what they preach, setting aside each Monday for a Family Home Evening.

The pamphlet went on to praise Mormon characteristics: industriousness, self-reliance, resistance to government interference. Stewardship, it said, "is one of the loveliest words in the English language." So is temperance, a rather fusty word unashamedly adopted by Mormons. They abjure not only alcohol, but also tobacco, coffee, tea, and soft drinks. In short, the Mormons point to upright living, high achievement, and sterling citizenship as primary proofs of their faith.

Despite the obvious appeal of all these qualities, something nagged at me as I read the pamphlet. The virtues it extolled brought to my mind not Mormons but evangelicals. Virtually every word could have been written by the National Association of Evangelicals in a brochure promoting evangelicals. Do we not want to be known for good citizenship, industriousness, righteousness, and temperance? If you took an on-the-street survey, asking strangers to "Describe an evangelical," you might get responses very similar to what is described in the Mormon brochure. Clean-living. Moral. Concerned about family. Ethical. Good things all. Evangelicals are, like

Mormons, the kind of people most Americans want to have as neighbors, but not spend too much time with.

One of Walker Percy's characters in *The Second Coming* captures well this typical attitude:

> Take Christians. I am surrounded by Christians. They are generally speaking a pleasant and agreeable lot, not noticeably different from other people — even though they, the Christians of the South, the U.S.A., the Western world, have killed off more people than all other people put together. Yet I cannot be sure they don't have the truth. But if they have the truth, why is it the case that they are repellent precisely to the degree that they embrace and advertise the truth? One might even become a Christian if there were few if any Christians around. Have you ever lived in the midst of fifteen million Southern Baptists? . . . A mystery: If the good news is true, why is not one pleased to hear it?

His last question rings loud. Could it be that Christians, eager to point out how good they are, neglect one basic fact — that the gospel comes as a eucatastrophe, a spectacularly good thing happening to spectacularly bad people? Wouldn't a phrase like Repentant Majority or Forgiven Majority serve as a more orthodox way of defining Christians than Moral Majority? Such a label would clearly credit God for any goodness, thus assuring that, in Paul's phrase, "no one can boast."

Since evangelicals have been busily reading into the *Congressional Record* biblical rationales on abortion, the Department of Education, tobacco subsidies, and sundry Supreme Court decisions, I would propose an important and corrective balance. In our churches, why not spend more time discussing the implications of Jesus' parable of the righteous man and the tax collector? One man thanked God for his blessings, that he was not a robber, evildoer, adulterer, or tax collector. He fasted twice a week and tithed his income. The other had an indefensible morality, not much in the way of a resume, and a thoroughly inadequate theology. One prayed eloquently; the other said seven simple words, "God, have mercy on me, a sinner." Yet which one went home justified?

Curiously, the righteous Pharisees had little historical impact, save for a brief time in a remote corner of the Roman Empire. But Jesus' disciples — an ornery, undependable, and hopelessly flawed group of men — became drunk with the power of a gospel that offered free forgiveness to the worst sinners and traitors. Those men managed to change the world.

No Right to Scorn

I happened to be in Washington, D.C., on a day when 300,000 gay rights activists gathered there to march. The October day was chilly, and gray clouds spit raindrops on the column of marchers snaking through the capital. As I stood on the sidelines directly in front of the White House, I watched a rather remarkable confrontation.

About forty policemen, many of them mounted on horses, had formed a protective circle around a small group of Christian protesters. Thanks to their huge orange posters featuring vivid renditions of hellfire, the tiny knot of true believers had managed to attract most of the press photographers. Despite being outnumbered by the gays 15,000 to 1, the protesters were yelling inflammatory slogans at the marchers.

"Faggots go home!" their leader screamed into a microphone, and the others took up the chant: "Faggots go home, faggots go home. . . ." When that got tiresome, they switched to "Shame-on-you-for-what-you-do." Between chants the leader delivered brimstone sermonettes about false priests, wolves in sheep's clothing, and the hottest fires in hell (which, he said, were reserved for sodomites and other perverts).

"AIDS, AIDS, it's comin' your way" was the last taunt in the protesters' repertoire, and the one shouted with the most enthusiasm. I, along with the protesters, had just seen a sad procession of several hundred persons with AIDS — some in wheelchairs, some with the gaunt and sunken faces of concentration-camp survivors, some covered with purplish sores. Listening to the chant, I could not fathom how anyone could wish that fate on another human being.

The gay marchers themselves had a mixed response to the Christians. The rowdy ones blew kisses or retorted, "Bigots! Bigots! Shame on you!" One group of lesbians got a few laughs from the press by yelling in unison to the protesters, "We want your wives!"

Among the marchers were at least 3000 who identified themselves with various religious groups: the Catholic "Dignity" movement, the Episcopalian group "Integrity," and even a sprinkling of Mormons and Seventh Day Adventists. Over 1000 marched under the banner of the Metropolitan Community Church (MCC), a denomination that professes a mostly orthodox theology except for its stance on homosexuality. This last group had a poignant reply to the beleaguered Christian protesters: they drew even, turned to face them, and sang, "Jesus loves you, this we know, for the Bible tells us so."

The abrupt ironies in that scene of confrontation stayed with me long after I left Washington. On the one side were "righteous" Christians defending pure doctrine (not even the National Council of Churches has deemed the MCC denomination worthy of membership). On the other were "sinners," many of whom openly admit to homosexual practice. Yet one side spewed out hate and the other sang of Jesus' love.

*   *   *

Another scene, one with haunting similarities to the confrontation in Washington, came to my mind. John 8 tells of a time when Jesus faced two contrary parties. (Although the passage is missing from the earliest copies of John, the story probably records an actual event.) On the one side stood "righteous" Pharisees and teachers of the law. On the other stood a condemned sinner, a woman caught in the act of adultery. The Pharisees had dragged her into the temple courts to set a trap for Jesus. Would he follow Mosaic law and order her execution by stoning — even though the Romans forbade it — or would he go against the Law?

In his masterful style, Jesus sprang the trap back on the accusers. "If any one of you is without sin," he said, "let him be the first to throw a stone at her." As Jesus stooped down and wrote on the ground with his finger, the fractious crowd filed silently away, all except the woman who had sinned. "Neither do I condemn you," Jesus said to her at last. "Go now and leave your life of sin."

For me, Jesus' response offers an important principle that applies to everyone, "righteous" and "sinner." To those tempted toward self-righteousness or smugness, Jesus gives a word of correction. He summons out into the open the sins we strive to keep hidden. We have no right to scorn and hate others, for we too are sinners.

Self-righteousness poses a special danger to people like — well, like strict Christians, who value correct doctrine and preach high moral standards. But it poses an equal danger to people like the MCC marchers, some of whom search diligently for biblical loopholes to excuse sexual promiscuity. For all of us the message is the same: bring to the surface sins that you would rather repress or rationalize away.

Jesus gave a strikingly different message to the obvious "sinner" in the story. To the woman caught in the very act, he offered not execution by stoning, but acceptance and forgiveness. There is no sin — not murder, not adultery, not homosexual promiscuity — powerful enough to exclude a person from acceptance by God. Only a refusal to repent stands between a sinner and God's free gift of forgiveness.

Joy Davidman used to say that Christians are not necessarily more "moral" than anyone else in the world, just more forgiven. What does a "forgiven" person look like? That is a question I have asked myself often since that day of conflict in Washington, D.C.

Growing Up Fundamentalist

During my childhood and adolescence in the Deep South, I often went to churches of the type usually branded fundamentalist. I realize the word "fundamentalist" is used in many ways, some good, some bad; to help place us on the subcultural grid, I should note that these folks worried about liberal tendencies at Bob Jones University. More, we had a mean streak when it came to race. I regularly heard from the pulpit that blacks — and that was *not* the word we used for them — were subhuman, cursed by God to be a "servant" race. Almost everyone in my church believed that Martin Luther King was "a card-carrying Communist." (Do they really carry cards, these Communists?)

And so when a friend asked me to fill out a survey

designed for "Adult Children of Fundamentalism," I felt appropriately qualified as a research subject. First came a series of statements to rate. I was asked to mark by each whether I agreed, strongly agreed, disagreed, strongly disagreed, or didn't know. Here are some sample statements:

- I have trouble getting close to other people.
- God is capricious.
- My body is ugly.
- The world is a bad place.
- I have difficulty having fun.
- Feelings are bad.
- I'm quick to judge others.
- I tend to think in either/or, black or white, right or wrong.
- Sex is bad.
- I'm afraid that I'm going to hell.

I dutifully checked off my responses to these and other statements (No, I'm not telling), and then proceeded to the open-ended portion of the survey. It was there that I ran into some surprises.

Has guilt been an issue for you? What type of things do you feel guilty about? Do you consider yourself a judgmental person? Yes, guilt has been an issue for me. I was brought up feeling guilty for such borderline activities as roller skating (too much like dancing), bowling (some alleys serve liquor), and reading the Sunday newspaper. Today, I could do any of those things with an unsullied conscience, but I often feel guilt about other matters. And yet as I filled out the survey I realized I have no lingering resentment against guilt. My answer to the last part of the question may explain why: Yes, I consider myself a judgmental person, and that's one of the things I feel guilty about. Guilt is the very thing that makes me aware of my judgmentalism, not to mention numerous other flaws.

Over the years, while my personal list of "what I feel guilty about" has changed dramatically, my attitude toward guilt itself has moved from irritation to appreciation.

How did fundamentalism affect your sense of self-esteem? In what ways do you feel superior/inferior to other people? My mind went back to scenes of piercing shame. Standing before a high school Speech class trying to explain why I wouldn't be able to go with them to view a movie version of *Othello.* Sitting on a garish red-and-white Youth for Christ Bible Club bus, piano-equipped, as it lazily circled the school grounds, stirring up scorn. Listening to a Biology teacher sarcastically explain to the class why my twenty-page term paper had failed to demolish Charles Darwin's 592-page *Origin of the Species.*

Shame, alienation, inferiority — these defined my adolescence. And yet, I asked myself, what permanent damage had they done? I may still suffer some psychological scars, but what of the alternatives? I think of the spoiled rich kids in my high school; they grew up not with shame and inferiority but with arrogance and superiority. In high school, I envied them; now, I pity them. I was "handicapped" by fundamentalism, yes. But the handicap ultimately worked in such a way as to make me "poor in spirit," a state which Jesus described as a prerequisite for inheriting the kingdom of God.

What were you taught about emotions? What effect do you think your fundamentalist upbringing has had on your ability to achieve emotional intimacy? How do you think fundamentalism shaped what you learned about sexuality? OK, I admit fundamentalism did some real damage here. In my youth I felt a curious schizophrenia about emotions. On the one hand, I learned at church to repress emotions: negative emotions, such as anger, led to sin; positive emotions, such as joy and happiness, led to pride, a sin of a different stripe. Yet at the same time, I had to constantly brace myself against the emotionalism of the church services. Revival speakers, having dangled before us visions of hellfire, would cajole us through endless repetitions of *Just As I Am* until every last inner spark of fear and guilt had ignited.

Even the harmful effect of that whipsaw approach to emotions, however, has been partially redeemed. Seared emotions, a deep sense of alienation, a tendency toward inwardness — the residual impact of these has actually helped my career in writing, which relies on the stance of an observer who somewhat enters in but mostly stands on the sidelines.

The survey on fundamentalism, after proceeding in like manner for five pages, concluded by asking me to summarize the positive effects in my life of having grown up in fundamentalism, and then the negative. For positive effects, I listed these:

- Biblical literacy
- A recognition of the seriousness of individual choices and behavior
- God-awareness

For negative effects, I listed these:

• Cultural illiteracy
• Residual judgmentalism
• Social isolation and limited life-experiences.

It didn't take long for me to determine which of the two lists has proved more important in forming who I am today. In fact, a funny thing happened as I filled out the survey. I had expected the exercise would, by prompting me to relive painful moments, bring to the surface unresolved anger and resentment. But when I reached the end, I was struck mainly with a sense of gratitude for my heritage.

"Why was this man born blind?" Jesus' disciples asked. He gave an answer at once incomplete and profoundly satisfying: "Neither this man nor his parents sinned, but this happened so that the work of God might be displayed in his life." That's a good lesson for all of us with "handicaps" — even the handicap of fundamentalism — to remember. I realized, when I had completed the survey, that my sense of gratitude traced back to the healing grace of God, not fundamentalism. For me, a proof of that amazing grace has been its ability to penetrate within a system that, at times, seems especially designed to perpetuate Ungrace.

Morbidly Healthy

William James, the Harvard philosopher and psychologist, subjected to scientific scrutiny the spiritual claims of converted alcoholics, saints, evangelists, and ordinary believers. He published his findings in 1902 in a book that became a classic: *The Varieties of Religious Experience*. After interviewing many Christians and reading the journals of many more, James came up with two overall classifications: "healthy-minded" and "morbid-minded."

Healthy-minded religion was booming in James's own day, when the turn of the century had just capped an era of unprecedented peace and prosperity. "Every day in every way the world is getting better and better" became a slogan for the times. Many believers thought Christ's promised kingdom on earth either had begun, or was about to begin. Some of the most vigorous strains of healthy-mindedness flourished in the very backyard of Harvard, as Boston Brahmins added the plinth of religion to the liberal optimism of Ralph Waldo Emerson. Buoyant new sects such as Christian Science burst on the scene, full of promise.

James contrasted these liberal optimists with morbid-minded "evangelicals," represented by the revivalists Jonathan Edwards, John Wesley, and Charles Finney. These sin-brooders described the world in apocalyptic terms and declared the only hope to be a "twice-born" experience that offered salvation to a fallen world.

After surveying the two groups, healthy-minded optimists and morbid-minded revivalists, James came away surprisingly impressed with the latter. He fully understood the appeal of the healthy-minded: they discounted or denied evil, sickness, and death. But these faiths did not account for all the facts, he concluded. Even their greatest prophets committed evil, got sick, and died, just like everyone else. At least the revivalists described a world that actually existed, one riddled with sin and suffering.

As I read William James's classic study in the light of modern times, I could not avoid wondering what conclusions a similar survey might produce today. Has a dramatic shift occurred in the religious categories James defined?

Who is morbid-minded today? It appears that liberal optimists have given way to liberal pessimists, almost across the board. In Congress, the political liberals shake their heads and wag their fingers over the Social Security crisis, gun proliferation, the greenhouse effect; meanwhile, their conservative counterparts try to convince us America is flourishing. Similarly, in religion it is the mainline churches who keep bringing up the dark, troublesome issues of world conflict and nuclear weapons. Within the evangelical tradition, too, the pattern holds: the more liberal, the more doleful. Read a couple issues of *The Other Side* and *Sojourners* if you doubt that.

Even as liberal optimists (forgive the labels — I know no other way to discuss these things) have abandoned optimism, a new breed of evangelicals has rallied to carry the flag. Now we have positive thinking and possibility thinking and health-and-wealth theology — more brashly optimistic than anything Emerson dreamed of — all being preached from evangelical pulpits and appearing on the evangelical publishers' best-seller list. Simply turn on any of the top five Christian television programs and compare the message to the healthy-mindedness described by William James.

A stunning reversal has taken place since 1902. The healthy-minded have become morbid and the morbid have become healthy-minded. I ask myself what has happened in our century to cause such a reversal. Has the world improved so much? Few would say so. Have such remarkable breakthroughs of faith occurred that now Christians in America (though, oddly, not in Sudan, Iran, China, or Sri Lanka) are somehow exempted from "the slings and arrows of outrageous fortune"? Some would argue that new and vigorous faith indeed has arisen in these latter days, but most pastors I know report no sudden declines in cancer, divorces, and child abuse among the members of their congregations.

What, then, has brought on such a reversal? Here, I

confess, I must fight back a wave of skepticism. Has evangelical theology adapted, I wonder, to a rise in economic
and social status? Has our faith become more healthy-
minded because we happen to be more successful at this
point in history, in this particular nation? Have we become conservative because, simply, we have more to con-
serve?

William James died in 1910, and before long most of
the healthy-minded faiths around him passed away too.
As James prophesied, they had not accounted for all the
facts. They were crushed by the terrible weight of World
War I, a monstrous fact that exposed the flaws in their
vision of humanity and the world. I hope and pray that
an even more ominous fact does not arise to smother the
healthy-mindedness that has swept evangelicalism in the
last few decades.

Part IV

Necessary Voices

How do you write or talk about theology in a society that still uses the theological words, but has changed their meanings?

If Christians have their own Christian publishers, Christian bookstores, Christian magazines, Christian ads, and Christian broadcasting networks, how do non-Christians ever come across Christian products?

What is a Christian product?

Why do we shake our heads and bemoan the dearth of Christians in art and culture when the nineteenth-century's best novelists (Tolstoy and Dostoyevsky) and two of the twentieth century's best poets (T. S. Eliot and W. H. Auden) were avowedly Christian?

How many of us read those four authors today?

How could we justify wasting time on fiction and poetry in a time like this anyhow?

Why do we still shake our heads and bemoan the dearth of Christians in art and culture even though one of the dominant authors of this century writes like a modern Amos or Isaiah? Why do so few Christians get around to reading Aleksandr Solzhenitsyn?

What do we read?

Why does so much great art come from circumstances of oppression? Which makes a better nurturing environment for a Christian author: a free society full of Christians or a hostile society full of non-Christians?

How do you write or talk about theology in a society that doesn't even know the theological words? What would a Christian book look like in a completely secular culture — say, Japan?

What do the Japanese read?

What will our contemporary Christian products look like fifty years from now?

Dastardly Deeds of Deflation

Every month Wall Street traders await with bated breath the latest figures on the lurking problem of inflation. But the opposite problem plagues writers: the currency of words suffers from centuries of relentless deflation. If you study etymology even casually, the phenomenon stands out, an overwhelming pattern of words leaking away meaning over time. They retrogress, seldom progress.

Take *silly*. Nobody wants to be called silly — it means fatuous, ridiculous. Ironically, the original Anglo-Saxon word meant one who was happy and blessed with good fortune. Similarly, the word *idiot* started out as a respectable derivative of a Greek word describing a person peculiar in a proper sense, meaning private and nonconformist. Eventually, the word became so peculiar (another deflated word) that no one wanted to be an idiot.

Or consider *sincere*. Scholars disagree, but some think this word derives from sculptors' use of the Latin phrase *sin cera,* meaning "without wax." Sometimes a deft worker of marble would use wax to patch over unsightly gouges or scratches in his finished work of art; a flawless, honest work that needed no such makeup was called *sincere,* without wax. Nowadays, however, salesmen and politicians hire consultants to learn how to appear "sincere." Sincerity has become a kind of image, an acquired demeanor bearing no relation to what is actually going on in the salesman's insecure, doubting interior.

Word deflation presents a formidable problem to writers, pastors, and all who rely on words to express Christian ideas, for theological words have lost as much air as any. Why have seventy-five new versions of the Bible sprung up in this century? Good old King James words simply have not held up well in our era of deflated language.

Pity, for example, once meant mercy, or clemency. It derives from the same root as "piety," and once described someone who, like God, compassionately reached out to help the less fortunate. Eventually the emphasis shifted from the pietistic giver to the object of pity, who was seen as weak or inferior. A similar deterioration occurred with *charity.* When King James translators pondered the concept of *agape* love so eloquently expressed in 1 Corinthians 13, they decided on "charity" to convey the highest form of love. Alas, both words have badly slipped. People who attempted to demonstrate pity or charity apparently did not measure up to the lofty standards of their words, and the language adapted accordingly. Now we hear the protests, "Don't pity me!" and "I don't want your charity!"

I have a favorite deflated word: *cretin*. Medically, cretinism describes a grotesque condition of thyroid deficiency characterized by stunted growth, deformity, goiter, scurfy skin, and (groan) *idiocy*. The condition first came to light in regions of the Alps and the Pyrenees, where drinking water did not contain enough iodine. Gradually, the word *cretin* encompassed "anyone with a marked mental deficiency." And this outright slander devolved from the Latin word *Christianus*. Hmm. This etymology business can hit close to home.

The few remaining hallowed words get dirtied up in modern usage. Listen to a few popular songs about *love*, and try to detect any similarity between what those lyrics describe and what is defined in 1 Corinthians 13. *Redemption* has survived, but mainly in the form of recycling centers. Modern culture even seizes a term like *born again* and commandeers it for used cars, perfumes, and football teams. Sadly, Christians are not devising strong new words to catch the leaking meanings. We look mostly to psychologists for our neologisms, so we hear ceaselessly about our "friendship" or "personal relationship" with God, even though, as C. S. Lewis points out in *The Four Loves*, that image least accurately describes the Creator-creature encounter.

A few words have kept their shine, though, and may survive a few more decades. One word has infiltrated so widely that it would be hard to kill off without a struggle. *Grace*, a wonderful theological word, has been unashamedly borrowed by all segments of society. Many people still "say grace" before meals, acknowledging that daily bread is a gift from God. We are *grateful* for someone's kindness, *gratified* by good news, *congratulated* when successful, *gracious* when hosting friends. A composer adds *grace* notes to the score, which good pianists learn to play *gracefully*.

The secular publishing industry comes closest to preserving the original meaning of the word in their policy of *gracing* issues. If you subscribe for twelve issues of a magazine, you may continue to receive a few extra copies even after your subscription has run out. These are *grace* issues, free of charge, undeserved, sent to tempt you to re-subscribe. They're *gratis* — there it is again.

My favorite use of the root word *grace* occurs in a Latin phrase: *persona non grata*. A person unwelcomed and unaccepted, in a nation or at a party, is a *persona non grata*, literally, a person without grace. Whenever I hear those six mellifluous syllables I think of a passage from 1 Peter in which the apostle is reaching for words to impress his readers with the splendor of their calling. "You are a chosen people," he says, "a royal priesthood, a holy nation, a people belonging to God. . . ." And then, "Once you were not a people, but now you are the people of God; once you had not received mercy, but now you have received mercy" (2:9-10). From *persona non grata* to God's favorites, objects of his undeserved grace. If those rich concepts still endure, maybe there's hope for the English language yet.

A Converted Imagination

"I know hardly any other writer who seems to be closer
. . . to the Spirit of Christ Himself," said C. S. Lewis about
the Scottish preacher and fantasy-writer George Mac-
Donald. Lewis also said, "I fancy I have never written a
book in which I did not quote from him," and credited
MacDonald's *Phantastes* with stimulating his own "conversion of imagination." Given the shelffuls of books in
tribute to C. S. Lewis, it's about time we paid some attention to the man Lewis freely acknowledged as "my
master."

MacDonald admirably combined a "secular" life as
a novelist and man of letters with his original calling as
a preacher of the gospel. He counted such notables as
Thackeray, Dickens, Arnold, and Tennyson among his

friends. On a trip to the U.S. in 1873 he packed lecture halls and made the acquaintance of Emerson, Longfellow, Whittier, Holmes, and Harriet Beecher Stowe. He even discussed with Mark Twain the possibility of coauthoring a novel, as a defense against the trans-Atlantic copyright piracy both of them were experiencing. (One can only imagine the results of such a collaboration!) Other friends included many of the pre-Raphaelite painters, his patroness Lady Byron, the eccentric critic John Ruskin, and Oxford mathematician Charles Dodgson (Lewis Carroll).

Although he lived in a time of great conflict between science and religion, George MacDonald saw no split between the "natural" and "supernatural" worlds. He confessed that in his youth "One of my greatest difficulties in consenting to think of religion was that I thought I should have to give up my beautiful thoughts and my love for the things God had made." Instead, he discovered that "God is the God of the Beautiful — Religion is the love of the Beautiful, and Heaven is the Home of the Beautiful — Nature is tenfold brighter in the Sun of Righteousness, and my love of Nature is more intense since I became a Christian. . . ." Such Christian naturalism served to enrich the sensory descriptions in his novels.

"To know a primrose is a higher thing than to know all the botany of it — just as to know Christ is an infinitely higher thing than to know all theology," MacDonald once said. And those who knew him saw what it meant to know Christ. MacDonald had a sunny, playful disposition. He fathered eleven children, then adopted two more when their mother found herself in dire financial straits. His household was filled with the laughter of children and the lively conversation of endless guests. (A frequent house guest of the MacDonalds, Lewis Carroll immortalized one of their daughters and a pet cat in *Through the Looking Glass*.)

A biography by William Raeper, Secretary to the George MacDonald Society, has mined a wealth of information. It reveals such trivia as MacDonald's major in college (chemistry!) and the fact that at age seventy-three he took up the study of Dutch and Spanish. Assessing MacDonald's literary worth, Raeper generously suggests that "the sum of his work is greater than its individual parts." Of the twenty-six novels, *Phantastes* and *Lilith* stand out as the most enduring. But Raeper's analysis pales next to the convincing literary profile offered by C. S. Lewis in a foreword to his anthology of MacDonald. Lewis values MacDonald not as a stylist — like many Victorians, he suffered from a syrupy didacticism — but rather as a myth-maker. And, to Lewis, the spiritual insights seen fleetingly in the novels but plainly in MacDonald's journal and collected sermons are unsurpassed.

Thanks to two compilations by Rolland Hein (*Life Essential* and *Creation in Christ*), MacDonald's sermons can still be read, in a condensed form more suitable to modern readers. MacDonald had a rocky pastoral career. Parishioners forced him from the pulpit because of his belief that hell serves as a kind of purgatory leading toward the ultimate reconciliation of all creation. Church authorities also worried about his belief that animals would have a place in heaven and questioned the subtle influence of German idealism on his theology.

By the end of his life, however, MacDonald had

survived such controversies and was welcomed and
loved as a visiting speaker in many British churches.
Reacting against the strict Calvinism of his youth (like
his character Robert Falconer, he was "all the time feeling
that God was ready to pounce on him if he failed once"),
he presented God as a loving, merciful Father. An idyllic
relationship with his own widowed father fed that image. MacDonald said about God, "It cannot be that any
creature should know Him as He is and not desire Him."
Confident that the goodness of God would one day
spread throughout the entire universe, he practiced a
kind of "optimistic fatalism" that shows, for example, in
a letter he wrote to console his wife on a private grief:
"Well, this world and all its beginnings will pass on into
something better."

Learning about MacDonald puts his sermons in an
entirely different light. The powerful words on grace,
freedom from anxiety, and the inexorable love of God
actually came out of a life full of hardship. For years
MacDonald wandered penniless around London, looking
for a job. He suffered constantly from tuberculosis,
asthma, and eczema. Two of his children died in their
youth. He proved unsuccessful in landing a university
teaching post, and the large sales of his novels rarely
translated into financial rewards — too many of the
copies were pirated editions. His family resorted to stag-
ing productions of *Pilgrim's Progress* (featuring Mac-
Donald himself as Greatheart) as a way to pay bills.

Such difficult trials only enhance the example of
faith left by one of our greatest devotional writers. The
novel *Phantastes* ends with the leaves of trees whispering,
"A great good is coming — is coming — is coming to

thee, Anodos." George MacDonald believed that with all his heart, and applied the lesson to his own life as well as to all of history.

The Risks of Relevance

One spring quarter I rode an elevated train twice a week on its screeching course south, eighty-five blocks in all. When I boarded, I shared the car with Yuppies, the men decked out in starched cotton shirts and three-piece suits, the women anomalously attired in business suits and running shoes (clutching their dress shoes in bags under their arms). Along the route various ethnic types joined us, headed for factory jobs just south of downtown. Then would come a thirty-block ride through the underbelly of Chicago — old houses sagging and peeling, with garbage piled high against them. A war zone, under siege. Young African-Americans with oversized radios roamed the train cars, hawking jewelry, incense, cigarettes, and children's toys.

At last I would transfer to a bus for my destination: the imposing Gothic towers of the University of Chicago. There, for the next two hours I would sit in a room with eleven others and study the poetry of T. S. Eliot. The poems, though written half a century before, still had a haunting immediacy about them. Chicago commuters, detached and silent, their faces seamed with tension, were the very characters Eliot had described in *The Love Song of J. Alfred Prufrock* and in his plays. His images of urban squalor also matched precisely what my train had just sped past. In one poem especially the strange expatriate from America changed forever the way this century looks at itself. People are still debating the meaning of *The Waste Land*, but that epic of confusion and despair came to define the mood of a generation between world wars.

It is hard for us today to fathom the shock waves that went out in T. S. Eliot's time when he, the premiere poet of despair and alienation, became a Christian. It was as if a Norman Mailer had converted — or a Saul of Tarsus. At first friends explained his conversion as "just an intellectual thing," a longing for order that led him to take refuge in the Anglican church.

Eliot acknowledged that anxiety about the future was a central factor in his conversion. The global problems of his day make modern times seem calm by contrast: Hitler, Mussolini, and Franco were spreading terror throughout Western Europe, while Stalin ravaged half a continent to the east. Eliot concluded that only the Christian faith could bring order to that chaotic world. But whatever his initial motivation, faith took root and came to dominate his thinking and his work. Here is how he put it:

To believe in the supernatural is not simply to believe that
after living a successful, material, and fairly virtuous life
here one will continue to exist in the best-possible substitute for this world, or that after living a starved and
stunted life here one will be compensated with all the
good things one has gone without: it is to believe that the
supernatural is the greatest reality here and now.

. . . I take for granted that Christian revelation is the
only full revelation and that the fullness of Christian revelation resides in the essential fact of the Incarnation, in
relation to which all Christian revelation is to be understood. The division between those who accept, and those
who deny, Christian revelation I take to be the most profound division between human beings.

How did Eliot's faith affect his writing? Some complained it ruined him, that the output of the fifteen years
after his conversion lacked the depth and genius of the
early works. Eliot began to wonder if there was any room
for art in a world gone mad. How could a responsible
Christian devote time to fiction or poetry? His own writing took an odd turn as he began accepting assignments
from the church. Virgina Woolf and Ezra Pound grum-
bled that their friend was turning into a priest. England's
artistic community watched in horror as the man who
was arguably the century's greatest poet wrote a play for
a church fundraiser, composed captions for a patriotic
exhibition of war photos, and tried his hand at Christmas
verse. These all seemed more important, more *useful* than
his rather lofty, abstract poems.

Finally, burdened by the world crisis, Eliot turned
away from poetry entirely, toward economics and soci-

ology. He had apparently lost faith in the power of art. He contemplated schemes for redistributing wealth. He met regularly with groups of Christian thinkers that included such luminaries as Dorothy Sayers, Alec Vidler, Karl Mannheim, Nevill Coghill and Nicholas Berdyaev. He wrote three books of urgent warning about the state of the West, calling for an actively Christian society to halt the decline.

Eliot saw a fatal flaw in modern humanism. Unless the values a nation lived by came from outside — from above, he said — they were vulnerable to any form of tyranny. (History was soon to prove him right.) To combat the threats, he proposed a "Community of Christians" that would serve as a kind of elite "Moral Minority." As he saw it, this gathering, comprising the most fertile minds from a variety of fields, would formulate Christian values for the society at large.

Following Eliot's lead, such groups did form, but their members could rarely agree on practical programs, or even whether it was desirable for them to discuss practical programs. Their common Christian commitment hardly guaranteed a consensus on social issues. (To appreciate the problem, imagine a Community of Christians formed of Jerry Falwell, the Pope, the Episcopal Bishop, Ann Landers, and Martin Marty discussing homosexual rights and abortion policies.)

T. S. Eliot's reflections on society make a fascinating historical study, for many of the same issues have resurfaced and are fiercely debated in the United States today. Is the Moral Majority in America a logical extension of Eliot's Community of Christians? Do Christians have a right to impose their values on a pluralistic society? If not, who can suggest an alternative set of values?

Few students, however, are poring over Eliot's commentary on society. His political and social theories now seem quaint and a bit fustian, and scholars treat them with mild bemusement or outright contempt. None of his many writings on politics and social theory remains in print. In fact, just to view them I had to visit the rare book room of the university library. There, my backpack was emptied of all but a pencil and a pad of paper, and I was granted two hours in which to examine the works that occupied one of our century's greatest minds for two decades. They were yellowed, musty books printed on the cheap paper of the war years. The irony struck me with great force: all over the world, students still pore over his poetry, mining the allusions, exploring the images and symbols — many of them deeply Christian — embedded there.

*   *   *

The hundredth anniversary of T. S. Eliot's birth occurred in 1988, offering a good opportunity to reflect on his career as a living parable of the enduring value of art. Visit a public library today and ask to see sample issues from 1960 of the following magazines: *Harper's*, *The Atlantic Monthly*, *The New Yorker*, *Esquire*. Count the proportion of articles that are "literary" in nature compared with those oriented around politics or pragmatic issues. Then go to the racks containing current issues of the same magazines. You will find a much smaller proportion of literary articles in the current magazines. Or, pick up socially concerned Christian magazines such as *The Other Side* and *Sojourners*, or even *Christianity Today*, and note how much space they devote to the arts, especially those works that have no overt spiritual or social message.

As a society, we keep turning from art toward more urgent, practical concerns. In a world facing economic and environmental crisis and the threat of global holocaust, who has time for poetry and literature? Shouldn't we instead be writing and reading about regional wars, global poverty, arms sales, and other "relevant" matters?

Whenever I am tempted by such thoughts, I remember the continuing influence of such Christian authors as Tolstoy, Dostoevsky, John Donne, Jonathan Swift, John Milton, and especially T. S. Eliot. (Donne similarly gave up writing poetry at the height of his career, in order to devote himself to his sermons, which are seldom read today. Milton abandoned poetry for twenty years during England's Civil War.) All of these wrote voluminously about the relevant issues of their time, and all those works have become mere curiosities, obscure footnotes to literary history. Meanwhile, their creations, based on, in Faulkner's words, ". . . the old universal truths lacking which any art is ephemeral and doomed — love and honor and pity and pride and compassion and sacrifice," have not ceased to illuminate and inspire.

Somewhere along the way, T. S. Eliot recovered his poetic voice. In a series of poems, *The Four Quartets,* written at the height of World War II, he managed to blend together the music and the message. These poems show the sharp, probing eye of the early work, but are tempered with insights from his religious pilgrimage. One sample:

> The wounded surgeon plies the steel
> That questions the distempered part;

Beneath the bleeding hands we feel
The sharp compassion of the healer's art
Resolving the enigma of the fever chart.

Our only health is the disease
If we obey the dying nurse
Whose constant care is not to please
But to remind of our, and Adam's curse,
And that, to be restored, our sickness must grow worse.

Like many Christians in the arts, T. S. Eliot questioned the inherent value of what he was doing. *Is art worth it? Is it useful enough?* At times it hardly seemed so, in light of global crisis. Yet perspective changes with the advance of time. I doubt there would even *be* a class on Eliot at the University of Chicago if all we had were his papers on social theory and his church plays. And I know I would not travel eighty-five blocks on an elevated train to attend such a class if it did exist.

In a world of fugitives the person taking the opposite direction will appear to run away.

— T. S. Eliot

Two Stubborn Calves

Joseph Frank's biographical volume, *Dostoevsky: The Years of Ordeal, 1850-1859*, focuses on the ten-year period that formed the character and spiritual outlook of one of the greatest novelists of all time. As I read this portion of the five-volume work, I could not help thinking of the many parallels between Feodor Dostoevsky, the literary giant of the nineteenth century, and Aleksandr Solzhenitsyn, a giant of our own century. Solzhenitsyn himself gave conscious tribute by naming the main characters in *One Day in the Life of Ivan Denisovich* after their prototypes in Dostoevsky's *The Brothers Karamazov*. Remarkably, both authors trace their spiritual development to a term of imprisonment in Siberia, where each experienced an unexpected religious conversion and endured a refiner's fire of suffering.

135

Dostoevsky underwent an almost literal resurrection. He was arrested for belonging to a group judged treasonous by Tsar Nicholas I, who, to impress upon the young parlor radicals the gravity of their errors, sentenced them to death and staged a mock execution. The conspirators were dressed in white death gowns and led to a public square. Blindfolded, with their arms bound tightly behind them, they were paraded before a gawking crowd and then tied to stakes before a firing squad. At the last instant, before the order to fire, a horseman galloped up with a prearranged message from the Tsar: he would mercifully commute their sentences to hard labor. Dostoevsky never recovered. He had peered into the jaws of death, and from that moment life became for him precious beyond all calculation. Believing that God had given him a second chance to fulfill his calling, he pored over the New Testament and the lives of the saints. After ten years, he emerged from prison with unshakable Christian convictions, as expressed in one famous passage, "If anyone proved to me that Christ was outside the truth . . . then I would prefer to remain with Christ than with the truth."

Aleksandr Solzhenitsyn gives a moving account of his own religious awakening in volume two of *The Gulag Archipelago*. He had often marveled at the love, patience, and longsuffering of persecuted Russian believers. One night, as Solzhenitsyn lay in a prison hospital bed, a Jewish doctor, Boris Kornfeld, sat up with him and related the story of his conversion to Christianity. That very night, Kornfeld was clubbed to death while sleeping. Kornfeld's last words on earth, writes Solzhenitsyn, "lay upon me as an inheritance." He began to believe again. Like Dostoevsky, Solzhenitsyn also experienced a form of resurrection. Against all odds he recovered from stomach cancer in the harsh gulag environment, a miracle that convinced him God had delivered him to bear witness through his work. Ever since, he has put in 14- and 16-hour days to complete his task.

Prison offered the two authors other "advantages" as well. Besides shaping religious outlooks, it provided a human environment rich in material for their writings. Dostoevsky was forced to live at close quarters with thieves, murderers, drunken peasants — men filled with hatred for the sophisticated gentry he represented. In that world, melodrama was more than a literary convention. Biographer Frank notes, "Life in prison camp gave him a unique vantage point from which to study human beings living under extreme psychic pressure, and responding to such pressure with the most frenzied behavior." Such closeup experience led to unmatched characterizations, such as that of the murderer Raskolnikov in *Crime and Punishment*. In prison Dostoevsky's liberal view of the inherent goodness in common man, colliding with the reality he found in his cellmates, crumbled. But over time, he also saw, in glimpses, proof of the image of God in those lowly prisoners.

Solzhenitsyn had an uncannily similar experience. Although he initially found fellow inmates repellent, he later learned to see them in a different light. "Now, when I have an urge to write about my neighbors in that room, I realize what its principal advantage was: never again in my life, either through personal inclination or in the social labyrinth, would I get close to such people. . . . However tardily, I nonetheless caught myself and realized I had always devoted my time and attention to people who fascinated me and were pleasant, who engaged my sympathy, and that as a result I was seeing society like the Moon, always from one side." He too emerged with a new view of humanity that would inform all his writings. He reflects, "It was only when I lay there on rotting prison straw that I sensed within myself the first stirrings of good. Gradually, it was disclosed to me that the line separating good and evil passes, not through states, nor between classes, nor between political parties either, but right through every human heart — and through all human hearts. . . . Bless you, prison, for having been in my life."

In different ways, both authors offer a startling refutation of an accepted dogma of their day, and ours: that human beings are altogether conditioned creatures, not autonomous, free individuals. Dostoevsky was imprisoned by an autocratic regime for the express purpose of punishment, not rehabilitation. Yet paradoxically he emerged as an incurable Russophile, obeisant to his government and wise to the excesses of his earlier idealism.

Solzhenitsyn, on the other hand, was sentenced for the express purpose of rehabilitation. Scientific socialism had devised the gulag as a massive instrument of reprogramming, in order to purge society of nonsocialist elements. Solzhenitsyn had, after all, criticized the great Stalin in a letter to a friend. Instead, this graduate became the single most eloquent voice against the regime that had tried to rehabilitate him. By irrefutably documenting a holocaust with no equal (he estimates that sixty million died under the Soviet regime — ten times Hitler's total), he changed the course of intellectual history in the latter half of this century.

Solzhenitsyn entitled his literary biography *The Oak and the Calf*, alluding to a Russian fable about a stubborn calf who, with seeming futility, keeps butting its head against a large oak tree. The calf persists for so long that eventually the tree topples over. Materialism, utopianism, and behaviorism in their extreme forms — whether from the West or the East — offer formidable challenges to a Christian doctrine of the nature of man. We are fortunate that a few stubborn calves in the last two centuries have continued the struggle.

The Rejected One

Shusaku Endo, who died in 1996, was that rarest of Japanese creatures: a lifelong Christian. In a country where the church constitutes less than one percent of the population, he was raised by a devout Christian mother and baptized at the age of eleven. Even more amazing, Endo, Japan's foremost novelist, wrote books with Christian themes that invariably wound up on national best-seller lists. He was something of a cultural hero in Japan, and even hosted a nighttime television talk show.

Endo's fiction won praise from such writers as John Updike and Graham Greene, and he was often mentioned as a candidate for the Nobel Prize for Literature. Nine of his novels have been translated into English, but his most popular book in the U.S. has been *A Life of Jesus,* his personal account of faith.

Growing up as a Christian in pre-war Japan, Endo felt a constant sense of alienation. Classmates sometimes bullied him for his association with a "Western" religion. After the war he traveled to France, hoping to pursue the study of such French Catholic novelists as François Mauriac and George Bernanos. But Lyon in 1949 hardly made him feel welcome: he was spurned this time on account of race, not religion. The Allies had cranked out a steady stream of anti-Japanese propaganda, and Endo found himself the target of much racial abuse.

Rejected in his homeland, rejected in his spiritual homeland, Endo underwent a grave crisis of faith. He spent several years researching the life of Jesus in Palestine, and while there made a transforming discovery: Jesus, too, knew rejection. More, Jesus' life was *defined* by rejection. His neighbors laughed at him, his family sometimes questioned his sanity, his closest friends betrayed him, and his countrymen traded his life for that of a terrorist. While on earth, Jesus seemed to gravitate toward other rejects: those with leprosy, prostitutes, tax collectors, paralytics, notorious sinners.

This new insight into Jesus hit Endo with the force of revelation. From his faraway vantage point in Japan, he had viewed Christianity as a triumphant, conquering faith. He had studied the Holy Roman Empire and the glittering Crusades, had admired photos of the grand cathedrals of Europe, had dreamed of living in a nation where one could be a Christian without disgrace. But now, as he studied the Bible, he saw that Christ himself

had not avoided "disgrace." Jesus was the Suffering Servant, as depicted by Isaiah:

> ". . . there were many who were appalled at him:
>   his appearance was so disfigured beyond that of any
>   man,
> and his form marred beyond human likeness . . .
> He had no beauty or majesty to attract us to him,
>   nothing in his appearance that we should desire him.
> He was despised and rejected by men,
>   a man of sorrows, and familiar with suffering.
> Like one from whom men hide their faces. . . ."

Many of Endo's novels center on that theme of rejection and suffering. *Silence,* his most famous, tells of
Christians in Japan who recanted their faith in the face of
the shoguns' brutal persecution. Endo had read many
thrilling stories about the Christian martyrs, but none
about the Christian traitors. How could he? None had
been written. Yet, to Endo, the most powerful message of
Jesus was his unquenchable love, even for — *especially* for
— people who betrayed him. One by one, his disciples
deserted him; yet still he loved them. His nation had him
executed; but while stretched out naked in the posture of
ultimate disgrace, Jesus roused himself for the cry,
"Father, forgive them, for they know not what they do."

Shusaku Endo believes that Christianity has failed
to make much impact on Japan because the Japanese have
heard only one side of the story. They have certainly
encountered the beauty and majesty. Japanese tourists
visit Chartres and Westminster Abbey and bring home
pictures of that glory. Japanese choirs and orchestras, like

their Western counterparts, now perform Handel's *Messiah* and Bach's *Mass in B minor.*

But somehow the Japanese have missed another message: the story of a God who makes himself powerless, of a Son of God who weeps as he approaches Jerusalem. According to Endo, Japan, a nation of authoritarian fathers, has understood the father-love of God, but not the mother-love, the love that forgives wrongs and binds wounds and draws, rather than forces, others to itself. ("O Jerusalem, Jerusalem, you who kill the prophets and stone those sent to you, how often I have longed to gather your children together, as a hen gathers her chicks under her wings, but you were not willing!")

It is not just Japan, I think, that needs to hear this two pronged message. We all need a reminder. Christianity has two great symbols to offer the world: a cross and an empty tomb. An empty tomb without a cross would miss the central message of the gospel. As Endo points out, other religions offer a powerful, eternal Divine Being; only Christianity offers a God who became a man and suffered and died. The Servant did not take on meaningless pain: "he was pierced for *our* transgressions, he was crushed for *our* iniquities." In the course of his life and death, Jesus took on the weight of every reject, every failure, every sinner.

But a cross without an empty tomb would be merely tragic. Plenty of good men and women have lived, and loved, and died. Only one has come back after death with a promise to conquer death forever, and to make all things new.

We worship a risen Christ. We worship a crucified Christ. Anything less is not enough.

Forward to the Past

The sky was overcast when I began my run on Saturday morning, and midway through my route the clouds opened, drenching me with a cold, shivery rain. I'm sure I made a miserable sight in the hardware store I stopped by on the way home. Water dripped messily from my clothes and hair as I pulled a wadded-up bill from my running shorts to pay for some insulation materials. This day was off to a bad start.

After showering, I ground fresh coffee beans, sipped two cups of the hot, steaming liquid, and decided to scrap the list of chores I had assigned myself. Instead, I would go to a movie. The Chicago Film Festival was underway, and I soon found myself in a theater watching *Following the Führer*, a film about the Third Reich directed by Erwin

144

Leiser. Twenty-five years after his famous *Mein Kampf,* Leiser was again assuming the terrible burden of a German artist: he was trying to come to terms with his country's love affair with Hitler.

To my surprise, Erwin Leiser himself, a stout man with a moustache, was attending the premiere. He introduced the film by explaining, in thickly accented English, why he had made it. "I had built *Mein Kampf* around newsclips of the big Hitler rallies. I showed the *spectacle* of the Reich that had attracted the German people. But as I watched these newsreels again and again over the years, I realized that they did not portray everyday lives. They did not show ordinary Germans. Yes, some people were screaming support for Hitler — but look at the newsreels. Other people stared straight ahead, with blank expressions. What about them? What was going on in their lives? I made this film in an attempt to answer that question."

Thus, in his second film on Hitler's Germany, Leiser tried to re-create everyday life. Once again he began with well-known newsclips: goose-stepping soldiers, huge outdoor rallies, the burning of the Reichstag building, scenes from the Krystallnacht of violence against the Jews. But in between these familiar scenes he spliced small, dramatized vignettes of life in Germany.

- A judge sits in a chair in a Nazi bureaucrat's office. He is stripped of all dignity. He squirms, and explains limply why he skipped a Nazi rally in order to play Mozart with his regular chamber orchestra.
- A cleaning woman who is scrubbing tile steps with Teutonic vigor stubbornly defies her neighbor's advice that she stop working for Jewish households.

- Disgruntled shoppers wait out a bombing raid in an underground shelter; they gossip about military defeats that have never made the German press.
- An army officer on Christmas leave spoils all his wife's attempts to create a festive mood. He empties a bottle of Christmas wine virtually at one gulp; it's the only way, he says, to forget about the cattle cars full of Jews he has shipped back from the Eastern front.
- Two teenage draftees come across a printed flyer dropped from an Allied plane. It shows corpses stacked like cordwood inside a German concentration camp. They argue: Can such things truly be happening or is it merely propaganda?

The film, by its technique of alternating newsclips and personal vignettes, explores the thick gray border between what will come clear to later history and what actually happens in everyday life. Now, looking back, the evils of Nazism loom large, and film footage of bombing runs, mass rallies, and concentration camps documents that evil. But at the time ordinary German citizens responded to those evils with small, quotidian choices made in a fog of confusion.

As I walked home from the film through a persistent drizzle, I thought about the banality of evil that Leiser had presented. We do not like to think of it as banal; we prefer our evil characters larger than life, like Adolf Hitler, who gives a face to the worst instincts of our species. Because of Hitler, we can take a kind of perverse comfort in the knowledge that someone is worse than we are; and thus, ironically, his horrible ex-

tremism may tempt us to discount our own lesser forms
of intolerance or idolatry.

* * *

The theater was a mile from my house, and as I walked
away, my thoughts turned closer toward home, to the
United States. What will *come clear* to filmmakers who
forty years from now will rummage through newsclips
of our time?

Will we be a shining beacon of freedom, a light on
the hill? Will we go down in history (or what's left of it)
primarily as the civilization whose weapons made
possible something unprecedented: the abolition of all
humanity? How will our million abortions a year look a
few decades from now?

Or, what if a filmmaker of the future avoids politics
entirely and simply assembles a montage of pop culture.
What would the future learn from a Madonna concert,
Garfield the Cat cartoons, Jane Fonda's videotapes,
Stephen King's novels? Will filmmakers include excerpts
from "Lifestyles of the Rich and Famous," or perhaps a
panorama of the frenzied high-tech stock exchange, as a
tribute to our great wealth?

What if one of the environmental nightmares we
keep hearing about so monotonously comes true — the
ozone layer breaks down, or the polar ice caps melt, or
acid rain kills off the last lake in North America? What
will *come clear* about our civilization then?

The more I conjectured, the more depressed I felt.
And when my thoughts turned inward and I wondered
how I, an ordinary citizen, fit into any of these scenes, I

felt even more depressed. How would an Erwin Leiser of the twenty-first century splice together scenes from my life with newsclips of these confusing times? I felt a sense of helplessness and doom such as I have not felt since the Sixties, when nearly everyone felt helpless and doomed.

When I arrived home, I took out a piece of leftover pizza from a cardboard box in the refrigerator and heated it in the microwave. Then I decided to do my list of Saturday chores after all. I spent the rest of the afternoon pressing flexible caulking around the windows in my house.

Part V

Life with God

What is God like? How is it that most theology books portray him as logical, orderly, unchanging, and ineffable whereas the Bible portrays him as emotional, flexible, vulnerable, and, above all, passionate?

Why is only about ten percent of the Bible — the Epistles — written in a straight didactic form while all the rest uses the more indirect forms of history, poetry, parable, and prophetic visions? Why are ninety percent of the sermons in evangelical churches based on the didactic ten percent?

How can God love so many people at the same time? If he does love us, why do some of our most urgent prayers go unanswered? Why aren't there more miracles?

Why is the book of Job in the Bible? Has anyone proposed an argument against a loving God that does not appear in some form in the book of Job? If Job emerges as the hero and his friends as the villains, why do Christians quote Job's friends more often than they quote Job himself?

Why didn't God answer Job's questions? Why didn't Job seem to care?

How can TV evangelists so buoyantly promote a health-and-wealth theology in a world as full of injustice and suffering as this one? Do any Iranian Christians believe in a health-and-wealth theology?

How can TV evangelists promise prosperity and security to the faithful even though Jesus promised them a cross, sent them out as lambs among wolves, and left most of his disciples to die martyrs' deaths?

What makes God happy?

The Jilted Lover

For two weeks one winter I holed up in a mountain cabin in Colorado. I brought along a suitcase full of books and notes, but at the end of the two weeks I found I had opened only one of the books: the Bible. I began at Genesis and read straight through. Outside, snow was falling furiously. By the time I reached Deuteronomy, snow covered the bottom step; when I hit the prophets, it had crept up the mailbox post; and when I finally made it to Revelation, I had to call for a truck to unbury the driveway. Over six feet of fresh powder fell during my time there.

The combination of snow-muffled stillness, isolation from all people, and singular concentration changed forever the way I read the Bible. Above all else, this is what struck me in my daily reading: Our common im-

pressions about God may be very different from what the
Bible actually portrays. In theology books you will read
of the decrees of God, and of such characteristics as omnipotence, omniscience, and impassibility. Those concepts can be found in the Bible, but they are well buried
and must be mined. Simply read the Bible and you will
encounter not a misty vapor but an actual Person. God
feels delight, and anger, and frustration. Again and again
he is shocked by human behavior. Sometimes, after deciding on one response, he "changes his mind."

I know, I know, the fancy word "anthropomorphism"
is supposed to explain all those human-like portrayals.
And yet if you read the Bible straight through, as I did, you
cannot help being overwhelmed by the joy and the anguish
— in short, the passion — of the Lord of the Universe. True,
God "borrows" images from human experience to communicate in a way we can comprehend, but surely those
images point to an even stronger reality behind them. In
the Prophets, for example, two images prevail: that of an
angry parent and that of a spurned lover.

To my surprise, Jeremiah affected me more than any
other book, probably because that prophet expresses
these two images of a passionate God with such emotional force. The early chapters of the book show an of-
fended parent trying to reason with a hopelessly rebellious child. God recounts how he led his children
through a hostile desert, providing food and water along
the way, to bring them into a fertile land of prosperity. "I
thought you would call me 'Father' and not turn away
from following me," he says (3:19). Instead, the nation
turned every direction but toward God. They went so far
as to practice infant sacrifice, something — an omniscient

God is speaking here — "I did not command or mention, nor did it enter my mind" (19:5; 7:31).

God's conversations with Jeremiah express the anger and futility, and behind them the pain, every parent feels on occasion. Suddenly, a lifetime of selflessly given love seems wasted, scorned. Deep family hopes wither and die. The child, bent on twisting a knife in the belly of his parents, defies them with shocking behavior, acting in such a way as "did not enter my mind."

Later, Jesus would use an even more primal image, from the animal kingdom, as he wept before a city that a few days later would commit a form of eternal patricide. "O Jerusalem, Jerusalem, you who kill the prophets and stone those sent to you, how often I have longed to gather your children together, as a hen gathers her chicks under her wings, but you were not willing!"

The Bible shows God's power to force a Pharaoh to his knees and reduce mighty Nebuchadnezzar to a cud-chewing lunatic. But it also shows the impotence of power to bring about what God most desires: our love. When his own love is spurned, even the Lord of the Universe feels in some way like a parent who has lost what she values most, or a mother hen who watches helplessly as her brood flees toward danger.

In Jeremiah the speeches shift, sometimes in mid-sentence, from the parental point of view to that of a lover. Again and again God uses the startling language of a cuckolded lover. He says of Judah,

> ". . . consider what you have done.
> You are a swift she-camel
>   running here and there,

a wild donkey accustomed to the desert,
sniffing the wind in her craving —
in her heat who can restrain her?" (2:23-24)

The tone of God's speeches in Jeremiah varies wildly, moving abruptly from these outraged cries of pain to warm entreaties of love, and then to desperate pleas for a new start. The wild swings of mood may be baffling — unless you've been through an experience such as God describes. He is responding like a jilted lover. A friend of mine endured two years of such pain. In November she was ready to kill her unfaithful husband. In February she had forgiven and moved back in. In April she filed for divorce. In August she abandoned the procedure and asked her husband to return. It took two years for her to face the truth that her love had been rejected forever, with no hope of healing.

The image of a wounded lover in Jeremiah (or in Hosea, where it is acted out in flesh) is an awesome one that I cannot comprehend. Why would the God who created all that exists subject himself to such humiliation from his creation? In Colorado, as I read through the pages of the Bible, I was haunted by the reality of a God who lets our response to him matter that much.

When I returned to Chicago, and started thumbing through theology books, I realized afresh a danger in our study "about" God. When we tame him, in words and concepts, and file him away under alphabetized characteristics, we can easily lose the force of the passionate relationship God seeks above all else. There may be no greater danger to those of us who write, talk, or even think about God. Mere abstractions, to him, may be the cruelest insult of all.

After two weeks of reading the entire Bible, I came away with the strong sense that God doesn't care so much about being analyzed. Mainly — like any parent, like any lover — he wants to be loved.

Mixed Metaphors

The book of Hosea is about spiritual adultery; no one who reads it can miss that. Hosea's wife, a slut named Gomer, reinforces the verbal message by graphically reenacting the story of Israel's infidelity to God. Yet, mysteriously, three-fourths of the way through Hosea a remarkable passage on parenthood sneaks in. For ten chapters God has expressed the jealousy and rage of a Jilted Lover, likening Israel to a woman who married him and then sold herself to other lovers. But in chapter 11 the tone dramatically alters.

> When Israel was a child, I loved him,
>   and out of Egypt I called my son. . . .
> It was I who taught Ephraim to walk,

taking them by the arms;
but they did not realize
    it was I who healed them.
I led them with cords of human kindness,
    with ties of love;
I lifted the yoke from their neck
    and bent down to feed them.

An image leaps into my mind from a videocassette
of a young girl learning to walk. The mother is on her
knees, coaxing forward her young daughter, who has
both hands extended and is rocking perilously from side
to side. The camera lurches wildly in the father's excitement. Both parents are grinning from ear to ear as they
play the tape over and over. Like that, like a doting parent,
God taught his people to walk. In this passage, he is
recalling the nostalgic joy of parenthood. "How can I give
you up, Ephraim?" he suddenly cries out in a stab of pain.
"How can I hand you over, Israel?" His heart is changed
within him; his compassion is aroused.

What can account for this tender interlude in the
midst of an adult story of seamy prostitution? Mixing the
two images — Israel as child, Israel as lover — is uncon-
ventional, to say the least. If a human speaker mixed those
two images, we would think of incest. But God, reaching
for any analogy to express his profound feelings for his
people, settles on the two deepest human relationships,
parenthood and marriage. As I puzzled over the extraordinary mixing of these images in Hosea, I settled on one
word, *dependence*, as the key: the key to what they have
in common and the key to how they differ.

For a child, dependence defines the relationship. A

baby depends on parents for her every need, and parents perform distasteful chores — staying up all night, cleaning up vomit, teaching toilet training — for they sense the child's dependence, and they love the child. With no parent to care for her, the child will die.

Yet such a pattern must not last forever; a good parent gradually nudges the child from dependence toward independence. My friends taught their daughter to walk, rather than pushing her around in a large carriage for life, although they knew full well she might one day walk away from them. Some parents, sadly, fail this test. I know a mother who keeps her 37-year-old son at home; she pockets his paycheck at the end of each week and insists that he ask her permission to go out. Anyone can sense their lack of health. In parenthood, dependence should flow toward freedom.

Lovers reverse the flow. A lover possesses freedom and yet chooses to give it away. "Submit to one another," says the Bible, and any couple can tell you that's an apt description of the day-to-day process of getting along. The romanticist Elizabeth Barrett Browning wrote this in a sonnet just before her marriage to Robert:

> And as a vanquished soldier yields his sword
> To one who lifts him from the bloody earth —
> Even so, Beloved, I at last record,
> Here ends my strife. If *thou* invite me forth,
> I rise above abasement at the word.
> Make thy love larger to enlarge my worth.

In a healthy marriage, one submits to the other voluntarily, out of love. In an unhealthy marriage, submission becomes part of a power struggle, a tug-of-war between competing egos.

*   *   *

God grieves in Hosea because Israel had disrupted the flow of dependence. In the wilderness God had nurtured Israel with the goal of bringing her to adulthood and the freedom of the promised land. But she seized that freedom, and like a rebellious child — like Gomer — flaunted it by running away from God. She never learned the meaning of marriage; she never learned to give herself voluntarily, in love, to God. Hosea records the deep sadness of God, who wanted a lover but found only a child.

The pattern of dependence can, I think, teach us much about God's design for the human race. As I read Hosea and its striking mixed metaphors, I had to examine my own life. Do I prefer the comfort of a "childish" relationship with God? Do I cling to legalism as a form of security, and a delusive way of getting God to "like me better"?

Is my love for God conditional, like a child's? If things go poorly, do I want to run away, or yell "I hate you!" Or is it more like a marriage partner's — the old-fashioned kind of marriage, in sickness or in health, for better or for worse, till death do us part (or, in this case, till death do us join)?

The progression in the Bible, and especially in Hosea, teaches me what kind of love God desires from me: not the clinging, helpless love of a child, but rather the mature, freely given love of a lover. Although both loves express a form of dependence, there is a vital difference between the two — the difference between parenthood and marriage, between law and Spirit.

"Do It Again!"

A friend, a sophisticated, urbane young woman, stopped
me the other day with some exciting news — exciting to
her, at least. She spent ten minutes re-creating for me the
first steps of her year-old nephew. He could walk! The
child tottered like a drunk, and grasped couches and
chairs to steady himself, but *he could walk!* His legs bent
at the knees, his feet shot out, and his body lurched in an
unmistakably forward direction.

At the time I was caught up in her blow-by-blow
account. But later, as I reflected on our conversation back
in the sober surroundings of my office, I realized how
bizarre we would have sounded to an eavesdropper. With
the utmost enthusiasm we had been marveling at a skill
already mastered by all but a very few of the ten billion

humans who have inhabited this planet. So he could walk
— everybody can walk. What was the big deal?

It struck me that infancy provides a rare luxury, a
quality of *specialness* that nearly vanishes for the rest of
life. Growing up is a ceaseless scramble for attention.
Teenagers stay up past midnight cramming for tests,
abuse their bodies in torturous athletic regimens, work
overtime to afford designer clothes, primp for hours in
front of mirrors — all for recognition. Adulthood merely
institutionalizes the mad rush for achievement. We want
desperately to stand out, to be noticed. Meanwhile, an
infant need only take a few herky-jerky steps across a
living room carpet and his parents and aunts brag about
the triumph to all their friends.

The limelight of special attention may re-ignite when
time comes for romance. To a lover every mole is cute,
every weird hobby a sign of lively curiosity, every sniffle
a cause for inordinate pampering. Once again we are
blessed with *specialness* — for a while, anyway, until the
tedium of life chases it away.

What happens during fawning parenthood and en-
rapt courtship offers a sharp contrast to our normal behavior. We do not step onto a bus and exclaim to the
driver, "I can't believe it! You mean you drive this great
big bus all day long, all by yourself! And you never have
an accident? That's wonderful!" We do not stop a fellow-
shopper in the supermarket aisle and gush, "I'm so proud
of you for knowing what brands to pick. There's a huge
variety, and yet you go right to the ones you want and
put them in your basket and push them around with such
confidence! Most impressive!" Yet that spirit, absurd
when applied to the humdrumness of life, is precisely

what we show toward children and lovers. For them, we "hallow" the ordinary and mundane.

I do not propose that we make fools of ourselves each time we come across a bus driver or a thrifty shopper. But thinking about our treatment of children and lovers did give me further appreciation for some biblical metaphors. More than any other word pictures, God chooses "children" and "lovers" to describe our relationship with him.

The Old Testament abounds with husband-bride imagery. God woos his people, and dotes on them like a lover doting on his beloved. When they ignore him, he feels hurt, spurned, like a jilted lover. The New Testament often uses the same imagery, picturing the church as "the bride of Christ." Shifting metaphors, it also announces that we are God's children, with all the rights and privileges of worthy heirs. Jesus (the "only begotten" Son of God) came, we're told, to make possible our adoption as sons and daughters in God's family. Study these passages, and you will see that God looks upon us as we might look upon our own child, or our lover.

Infinity gives God a capacity we do not have: he can treat all of creation with unrelieved specialness. G. K. Chesterton put it this way:

> A child kicks his legs rhythmically through excess, not absence of life. Because children have abounding vitality, because they are in spirit fierce and free, therefore they want things repeated and unchanged. They always say, "Do it again"; and the grown-up person does it again until he is nearly dead. For grown-up people are not strong enough to exult in monotony. But perhaps God is strong

enough to exult in monotony. It is possible that God says every morning, "Do it again" to the sun; and every evening, "Do it again" to the moon. It may not be automatic necessity that makes all daisies alike; it may be that God makes every daisy separately, but has never got tired of making them. It may be that He has the eternal appetite of infancy; for we have sinned and grown old, and our Father is younger than we.

As I read the Bible, it seems clear that God satisfies his "eternal appetite" by loving individual human beings. I imagine he views each halting step forward in my spiritual "walk" with the eagerness of a parent watching a child take the very first step. And perhaps, when the secrets of the universe are revealed, we will learn an underlying purpose of parenthood and romantic love. It may be that God has granted us these times of *specialness* to awaken us to the mere possibility of infinite love. Of that love, our most intimate experiences here on earth are mere glimpses.

Thoughts about Jesus While
Standing in a Dilapidated Diner

On one of Chicago's coldest, dreariest winter nights, I found myself standing inside a dilapidated diner, waiting for a tow truck. My car's engine had died in an intersection. As I stood in the diner, shivering and wasting time, I could not help thinking of a story about Jesus I had just been reading.

I had come across one of the most fanciful of the apocryphal Gospels, the *Gospel of the Infancy of Jesus Christ*. This early church document, accepted by no church as canonical, purports to reveal unknown stories from Jesus' childhood, a period virtually passed over in the canonical Gospels. It tells of the boy Jesus shaping birds out of clay and then watching delightedly as they flap away, alive. It shows him breaking a witch's spell that had trans-

167

mogrified a man into a mule. Where Jesus' sweatdrops hit the ground, balsam trees grew; where his swaddling clothes lay, fire did not burn. A dying boy placed in Mary's house was cured by the mere smell of Jesus' garments.

The apocryphal Gospel made me grateful for the contrastingly sober reporting of the canonical writers. In them, miracles are not magic or caprice, but rather acts of mercy or *signs* pointing to underlying spiritual truth. One of the apocryphal stories from Jesus' childhood has stayed with me, however. It has a certain charm — partly, I think, because it so closely parallels a view of Jesus widespread in some Christian circles today. It was this story that came to mind as I waited in the diner for a tow truck.

According to the *Gospel of the Infancy,* Jesus' father Joseph was a mediocre carpenter. He would do his best to fashion milk pails, gates, sieves, and boxes in his workshop, and then would call upon Jesus for the final touch. Whereupon Jesus would stretch out his hand, and miraculously Joseph's workmanship would expand or contract to just the right shape, and smooth to just the right finish. On one especially crucial job, the story goes, Joseph failed to measure correctly. He carved and beveled for months on an elaborate throne for a king, only to find it did not fit the required space. Enraged, the king muttered threats against Joseph. Just as things got tense, young Jesus appeared and, miraculously, the huge throne enlarged to fill the space. All the decoration stayed in perfect proportion as the throne expanded.

Oh, how I wish Jesus operated like that today! I say this not in sacrilege or in jest. As a freelance writer, I could desperately use his assistance. If I came up with the germ idea of an article and sketched out some rough copy, then Jesus could come along and scratch out dangling clauses and showy adverbs and unnecessary diversions of thought. One summer I worked for six weeks on articles designed to present a Christian message to a secular audience. I labored over every word, cutting and polishing, seeking the precise tone the magazine called for. But, like Joseph's throne, my articles came up short. Unlike Joseph, I experienced no miraculous intervention, and all my effort went to waste.

And now my car was sitting in the middle of Clark Street sending out SOS signals with its emergency flasher. I would miss a scheduled meeting that night and probably hours of work over the next few days as I tried to wring honest workmanship out of a service station set up to prey upon stranded motorists. What possible good could come from hours of haggling with a larcenous repairman? One slight miraculous adjustment to a timing belt and I could be on my way again, with more money in my pocket to give to worthy causes.

I know very well that choosing appropriate adverbs and keeping a car running are mere trivialities compared to the trials many Christians face each day. I think of those imprisoned for their faith overseas, and my friend with a mentally handicapped child. Why doesn't God reach down and fix them? The issue is not a belief in miracles. God surely has the power; why doesn't he use it?

Such a cosmic question hardly belongs in a chapter of this length, except as it touches on an important lesson to be drawn from the apocryphal Gospel. That Gospel, a favorite of second-century Gnostics, was properly rejected by the orthodox church. Its stories of Jesus' boy-hood express a dangerous heresy: the belief that we can escape this flawed material world, bound in time and space, and achieve life on a more "spiritual" plane, far above the tedium of everyday living.

The Apostle Paul battled Gnosticism valiantly. He clung to the promise of a perfect world to be granted us someday, of which we have a foretaste in this life. But he never denied the tedious, often painful realities of this life. How could he, with his days so full of shipwrecks, imprisonments, beatings, and the nagging pain of his mysterious "thorn in the flesh"? In short, Paul portrays the Christian life as a kind of suspension that includes the triumph of eternal victory but also the poignant "not yet" of our current state.

I confess, sometimes I wish it were not so. When I labor over a knotty article or try to coax a balky car to run, or when I face an intractable problem that will not go away — at such moments I yearn for a way to speed up the "not yet." I long for the messiah portrayed in the apocryphal Gospel, one who will hover beside me, fixing up my words, my physical flaws, and all the misfortunes of my life.

But then when I study the canonical Gospels, and the explanatory epistles that follow, I can see the wisdom in God's plan. It would be miracle, surely, for Jesus to stretch thrones, make clay birds fly, and change mules into men. But it is miracle far greater for him to take the ragtag group of eleven who followed him, along with an imperious Christian-hunter named Saul, and transform them, flaws and all, into the foundation of his Kingdom.

It would be miracle if all my words came out perfect

and if my car never failed again. *(I could accomplish so much more for the Kingdom, a voice whispers. . . .)* But that he uses the raw material of anything that I write, or that you say, or that we, his Body, accomplish on this earth — is that not greater miracle?

The Spirit of Arranged Marriages

Have you ever thought about how heavily our Gross National Product depends on romantic love? It dominates the arts: turn on any pop music station and try to find a song that does *not* feature that theme. In publishing, Gothic romances outsell every other line of books. And is there a television soap opera or comedy without a steamy romance woven into the plot? Entire industries exist to capitalize on romantic love: the fashion, jewelry, and cosmetic trades all tempt us to perfect techniques of attraction between man and woman. Phrases like "catching a man" and "hunting a woman" have come to summarize a fact of life in our culture and, we assume, in every culture. This is the way life is, we think.

Ah, but herein lies a remarkable phenomenon: still

today, in our international global village, over half of all marriages occur between a man and woman who have never felt a twinge of romantic love and might not even recognize the sensation if it hit them. Teenagers in most parts of Africa and Asia take for granted the notion of marriages arranged by parents in the same way we take for granted romantic love.

A modern young Indian couple, Vijay and Martha, explained to me how their arranged marriage came about. Vijay's parents pondered all the young girls in their social circle before deciding on one named Martha for their son to marry. Vijay was 15 then, and Martha had just turned 13. The two teenagers had met, briefly, only once before. But once Vijay's parents had reached their decision, they met together with Martha's parents and agreed on a wedding date eight years away. After all arrangements had been made, the parents informed both teenagers whom they would be marrying, and when.

During the next eight years, Vijay and Martha were permitted to exchange one letter a month. They saw each other on two — only two — closely chaperoned occasions before the wedding day. Yet, although they moved in together as virtual strangers, today their marriage appears to be as secure and loving as any I have known. In fact, missionaries who live in such societies report that as a rule arranged marriages have more stability and a much lower divorce rate than marriages resulting from romantic love.

In the U.S. and other Western-style cultures, people tend to marry because they are attracted to another's appealing qualities: a fresh smile, wittiness, a pleasing figure, athletic ability, a cheerful disposition, charm. Over time, these qualities can change; the physical attributes, especially, will deteriorate with age. Meanwhile, surprises may surface: slatternly housekeeping, a tendency toward depression, disagreements over sex. In contrast, the partners in an arranged marriage do not center their relationship on mutual attractions. Having heard your parents' decision, you accept that you will live for many years with someone you now barely know. Thus the overriding question changes from "Whom should I marry?" to "Given this partner, what kind of marriage can we construct together?"

*   *   *

I doubt seriously that the West will ever abandon the notion of romantic love, no matter how poorly it serves as a basis for family stability. But in my conversations with Christians from different cultures I have begun to see how "the spirit of arranged marriages" might transform other attitudes. We may have something to learn in our practical expectations of the Christian life, for example.

I have always found strange the modern theological fixation with the problem of suffering. People in our society live longer, in far better health, with less physical pain than any in history. And yet our artists, playwrights, philosophers, and theologians stumble over themselves in search of new ways to rephrase the ancient questions of Job. Why does God allow so much suffering? Why doesn't he intervene? Significantly, the outcries do not come from the Third World — where misery abounds — or from such persons as Solzhenitsyn who endured great suffering. The cry of anguish comes primarily from those of us in the comfortable, narcissistic West. In thinking through this odd trend, I keep coming back to the parallel of arranged marriages. It has become for me a parable of how different people relate to God.

Some people approach faith primarily as a solution to their problems, and choose God much like one would choose a spouse — by looking for desirable qualities. They expect God to bring them good things; they tithe because they believe their money will come back tenfold; they try to live right because they believe God will prosper them. These people interpret the phrase "Jesus is the answer" in its most literal, inclusive sense. The answer to what: Unemployment? A retarded child? A crumbling marriage? An amputated leg? An ugly face? All of the above. They count on God to intervene on their behalf by arranging a job for them, curing the retarded child and amputated leg and ugly face, and patching together the marriage.

And yet we must keep raising the problem of suffering, precisely because life does not always work out so neatly. In many countries, in fact, becoming a Christian guarantees a person unemployment, family rejection, societal hatred, and even imprisonment.

In her wonderful book *The Mind of the Maker*, Dorothy Sayers suggests another way of viewing God's involvement with us. She says, in words that merit much reflection, "The artist does not see life as a problem to be solved, but as a medium for creation." We are like artists who have been given the assignment of constructing our lives from a lump of raw material. Some of us are ugly, some beautiful, some brilliant, some dense, some charming, some shy. God does not promise to solve all the "problems" we have, at least not in the manner we may wish them to be solved. Rather, he calls us to trust him, and to stay faithful — whether we are affluent Americans or Sudanese Christians locked in prison. What matters most is what we create from the raw material.

In this view, we need "the spirit of arranged marriages" in our relationship with God. God made me the way I am: with my peculiar facial features, my handicaps and limitations, my body build, my mental capacity. I can spend my life resenting this quality or that one, and demanding that God change my "raw material." Or I can humbly accept myself, flaws and all, as the raw material God can work with. I do not go in with a list of demands that must be met before I take the vow. Like a husband in an arranged marriage, I precommit to Him regardless of how it may work out. There is risk. I am unsure of what the future will hold.

You might say that faith means taking a vow "for better or worse, for richer or poorer, in sickness or health" to love God and cling to him *no matter what.* Happily, "the spirit of arranged marriage" works two ways: God also precommits to me. Faith means believing he has taken that same vow, and Jesus Christ offers the proof. God does not accept me conditionally, on the basis of my performance. He keeps the vow, and therein is grace.

Job and the Riddles of Suffering

"But those who suffer he delivers in their suffering; he speaks to them in their affliction" (Job 36:15).

"Why me?" Almost everyone asks that question when suffering strikes. In circumstances large and small — an earthquake in South America or a diagnosis of illness — we face anguished questions about why God allows pain.

Ironically, suffering Christians often gain help and comfort from the book of Job. I say "ironically" because Job raises more questions about suffering than it answers. The conclusion of the book, which features a dramatic personal appearance by God himself, seems perfectly stage-managed for an enlightening monologue; but God avoids the question entirely. And various theories about the origin of suffering, fine-sounding theories proposed by Job's friends, God dismisses with a scowl.

The book of Job, an amazing account of very bad things happening to a very good man, thus contains no compact theory of why good people suffer. Nevertheless, it does offer many "over-the-shoulder" insights into the problem of pain. My own study has led me to the conclusions that follow. They do not answer the problem of pain — not even God attempted that. But these principles do shed light on certain misconceptions as widespread today as they were in Job's time.

1. Chapters 1 and 2 make the subtle but important distinction that God did not directly cause Job's problems. He permitted them, but Satan acted as the causal agent.

2. Nowhere does the book of Job suggest that God lacks power or goodness. Some people (including Rabbi Kushner in his best-seller *When Bad Things Happen to Good People*) claim that a weak God is powerless to prevent human suffering. Others deistically assume he runs the world at a distance, without personal involvement. But the book of Job does not call into question God's power, only his fairness. In the final summation speech, God uses splendid illustrations from nature to demonstrate that power.

3. Job decisively refutes one theory: that suffering always comes as a result of sin. The Bible supports the general principle that "a man reaps what he sows," even in this life (see Pss. 1:3; 37:25). But other people have no right to apply that *general* principle to a *particular* person.

Job's friends persuasively argued that Job deserved such catastrophic punishment. However, when God rendered the final verdict he said to them, "You have not spoken of me what is right, as my servant Job has" (42:7).

(Later, Jesus would also speak out against the notion that suffering automatically implies sin [see John 9:1-5 and Luke 13:1-5]). Having no clearly formed belief in an afterlife, Job's friends wrongly assumed that God's fairness — his approval or disapproval of people — had to be demonstrated in this life only.

4. God did not condemn Job's doubt and despair, only his ignorance. The phrase "the patience of Job" hardly fits the stream of invective that poured from Job's mouth. Job did not take his pain meekly; he cried out in protest to God. His strong remarks scandalized his friends (see, for example, 15:1-16), but not God.

Need we worry about somehow insulting God by an outburst that comes from stress or pain? Not according to this book. In a touch of supreme irony, God ordered Job's friends to seek repentance from Job himself, the object of their pious condescension.

5. No one has all the facts about suffering. Job concluded he was righteous but God was unfair. His friends insisted on the opposite: God was righteous and Job was being rightfully punished. Ultimately, all of them learned they had been viewing the situation from a very limited perspective, blind to the real struggle being waged in heaven.

6. God is never totally silent. Elihu made that point convincingly, reminding Job of dreams, visions, past blessings, even the daily works of God in nature (chapter 33). God similarly appealed to nature for evidence of his wisdom and power. Although God may seem silent, some sign of him can still be found. Author Joseph Bayly expressed the same truth this way, "Remember in the darkness what you have learned in the light."

7. Well-intentioned advice may sometimes do more harm than good. The behavior of Job's friends gives a classic example of how pride and a sense of being right can stifle true compassion. The friends repeated pious phrases and argued theology with Job, insisting on their wrongheaded notions about suffering (notions that, in fact, still haunt the church). Job's response: "If only you would be altogether silent! For you, that would be wisdom" (13:4-5).

8. God refocused the central issue from the *cause* of Job's suffering to his *response*. Mysteriously, God never gave his own explanation of the problem of suffering, nor did he inform Job of the the contest recorded in chapters 1 and 2. The real issue at stake was Job's faith: whether he would continue to trust God even when everything went wrong.

9. Suffering, in God's plan, can be redeemed, or used for a higher good. In Job's case, a period of great travail was used by God to win an important, even cosmic, victory. Looking backward — but only looking backward — we can see the "advantage" Job gained by continuing to trust God. Through his undeserved suffering, Job gave an "advance echo" of Jesus Christ, who would live a perfect life, yet endure pain and death in order to win a great victory.

*   *   *

Thousands of years later, Job's questions have not gone away. People who suffer still find themselves borrowing Job's words as they cry out against God's apparent lack of concern. But the book of Job affirms that God is not deaf to our cries, and is in control of this world no matter how it appears. God did not answer all the questions, but his very presence caused Job's doubts to melt away. Job learned that God cared about him, and that he rules the world. It was enough.

The Hardship Ladder

The German pastor/theologian Helmut Thielicke once observed that "American Christians have an inadequate theology of suffering." Who could disagree? More, how could we expect a theology of suffering to emerge from a society that has survived nearly two centuries without a foreign invasion, solves all meteorological discomfort with "climate control," and prescribes a pill for every twinge of pain?

At least part of our difficulty may come from how we read the Bible. I have found at least five biblical approaches to suffering, and if we focus on one of these approaches exclusively, we risk not only an inadequate but a heretical theology of suffering. I call the five stages the Hardship Ladder.

Stage 1: A person living right should never suffer. We have such "prosperity gospel" thoughts almost as a reflex. A 30-foot golf putt rims the cup but does not fall: "You must not be living right!" A youthful Christian leader comes down with cancer: "How could it happen to such a saint?" I acknowledge that such sentiments do appear in the Bible, especially in the book of Proverbs, which implies that right living will earn its reward *in this life.* And consider the sweeping promise of Psalm 1:3 to the righteous man: "Whatever he does prospers."

You would have to go back to Exodus and Deuteronomy to understand the source of this theology: God's covenant with the Israelites. God had guaranteed prosperity if the people would follow him faithfully, but the Israelites broke the terms of that covenant. Other biblical books, notably the prophets and Psalms, record the Jews' anguished adjustments to new realities. Almost a third of the psalms, for example, show a "righteous" author struggling with the failure of prosperity theology. It simply no longer seemed to work.

Stage 2: Good people do endure hardships, but they will always get relief. Many of the "hardship psalms" have about them a shrill tone of self-defense. The author seems to believe, "If I can just convince God of my righteousness, then God will surely deliver me. There must be some mistake involved."

I have come to see such "self-righteous" psalms as psalms of preparation. They help an entire nation understand that sometimes righteous people do suffer, and sometimes they don't get delivered. In that sense, these psalms are truly messianic: they prepare the way for Jesus, a perfect man who, as Hebrews says, "offered up

prayers and petitions with loud cries and tears to the one
who could save him from death." But Jesus was not saved
from death.

Hebrews 11 compiles a list of faithful persons
through the centuries. Some received miraculous deliverance: Isaac, Joseph, Moses, Rahab, Gideon, David. But
others were tortured and chained, stoned, and sawed in
two. The chapter gives vivid details about the latter
group: they went about in sheepskins and goatskins, were
destitute, wandered in deserts and mountains and in
holes in the ground. The author concludes with the blunt
assessment: "These were all commended for their faith,
yet none of them received what had been promised."

Stage 3: All things work together for good. That famous
phrase from Romans 8 is often distorted. Some people
think it means "Only good things will happen to those
who love God." Ironically, Paul meant just the opposite.
In the remainder of the chapter, he defines what kind of
"things" he is talking about: trouble, hardship, persecution, famine, nakedness, danger, sword. Paul endured all
those things, and in the end succumbed to them. He was
not "delivered." Yet, he insists, *"in all these things* we are
more than conquerors"; no amount of hardship can separate us from the love of God.

Paul found a neat way to resolve the contradictions
raised by the first two hardship stages. Even though hardships will afflict those who love God, they can see that
the condition is temporary. One day, when the "groaning"
creation is liberated at last, all hardship will be abolished.
We have a timing problem, Paul says. Just wait: God's
miracle of transforming Bad Friday into Easter Sunday
will be enlarged to a cosmic scale.

Stage 4: Faithful people may be called to suffer. The book of 1 Peter explains this new twist on hardship. Far from stage 1, where the righteous expect an immunity from suffering, this theology assumes persecution. Those believers following "in his steps" will, like Christ, suffer unjustly. History bears out Peter's words. Most of the apostles died martyrs' deaths, and the spilled blood of such martyrs became the seed for the church's growth.

Stage 5: Holy indifference. The apostle Paul reached the exalted state described in a passage like Philippians 1; Paul can hardly decide whether it's better to die and be with Christ or to stay a while and continue his ministry. His values seem topsy-turvy. Clearly, his stint in prison he sees as desirable, for that "hardship" has brought about many good results. Wealth, poverty, comfort, suffering, acceptance, rejection, even death or life — none of these circumstances matters much to Paul. Only one thing matters ultimately: the surpassing goal of exalting Christ, a goal which can be accomplished in any set of circumstances.

*   *   *

It bothers some people, I know, to list a series of biblical "stages" without a tidy formula resolving them into a grand scheme. For such people, I simply recommend contemplating stage 1 in the light of stage 5. Curiously, Paul's advanced state of holy indifference to pain puts him right back in stage 1. For Paul, a person living right did not suffer — not in any permanent sense, at least. And God could use all the events of Paul's life, whether painful or pleasurable, as a tool to advance his kingdom.

I have met few people who have attained the lofty state of stage 5, which may confirm Helmut Thielicke's comment about America. How can a nation so singularly blessed be expected to master advanced faith? We must turn instead to the Christians in El Salvador, or South Africa, or North Korea, for a lesson in the graduate school of suffering. Alas, it seems we devote more time and energy debating the possibilities of stage 1 — or at least yearning for those "good old days" when America won all its wars and the economy soared.

God Plays Favorites

The apostle John wrote, in the prologue to his Gospel, "No one has ever seen God, but God the only Son, who is at the Father's side, has made him known." Another sentence, in his first epistle (4:12), begins exactly the same, "No one has ever seen God," but follows with this astonishing assertion: ". . . but if we love each other, God lives in us and his love is made complete in us." Older translations render the phrase, accurately, "his love is perfected in us." It is a rather staggering notion that God has chosen ordinary people as the preferred medium to express his likeness — his love — to the world.

Yet the world God loves may never see him; our own faces may get in the way. I have long been disturbed by Dorothy Sayers' comment about God's three greatest

187

humiliations. The first humiliation, she said, was the Incarnation, when God took on the confines of a physical body. The second was the Cross, when he suffered the ignominy of death by public execution. The third humiliation is the church.

When I first read her comment, historical images came to mind: the Crusades, pogroms against the Jews, the Wars of Religion, slavery, the Ku Klux Klan. All these movements claimed Christ's sanction (one slave ship even sailed under the name *The Good Ship Jesus*). But the humiliation continued in our century in places like the former Yugoslavia, South Africa, Lebanon, and Northern Ireland, where some of earth's meanest conflicts involved Christians. Closer to home, I need only examine my own life to see the extent to which God humbles himself by dwelling within ordinary people.

Sadly, the watching world judges God himself by the actions of those who bear his name. Charles Swinburne's poem "Before a Crucifix" describes the "man-eating beasts" that prowled around the tree of faith and kept him from belief:

> Though hearts reach back and memories ache,
> We cannot praise thee for their sake.

Nietzsche said bluntly, "His disciples will have to look more saved if I am to believe in their Savior." The church is indeed God's humiliation, making the world safe for hypocrisy.

*   *   *

Although we cause God humiliation, we also bring him pride. Lately I have been noticing a few fascinating phrases that convey God's sense of pride, even delight, in people who remain faithful to him. I reviewed those passages, searching for characteristics common to God's "favorites." For example, the Angel Gabriel told the prophet Daniel to his face that he was "highly esteemed" in the heavens. In a speech to Ezekiel (chapter 14), God himself confirmed the judgment, listing Noah, Daniel, and Job as three of his favorites. Those three make for an interesting trio: one survived a flood, one a lion's den, and one a personal holocaust of suffering.

In fact, I noted that most of God's favorites underwent a severe test of faith. There was Abraham, called "a friend of God," who spent most of his life waiting impatiently for God to keep his promises. The Virgin Mary, too, "found favor with God," but, as Kierkegaard reminds us, "Has any woman been as infringed upon as was Mary, and is it not true here also that the one whom God blesses he curses in the same breath?" In *Fear and Trembling,* Kierkegaard expounds on the anxiety, distress, and paradox that marked Mary's life.

Of course, the Bible points to Jesus as the one in whom God took most pride. "This is my Son, whom I love; with him I am well pleased," said a voice like thunder from heaven. He, the Suffering Servant, surely fits the pattern; it was Jesus, after all, who embodied the other two great humiliations of God.

The same pattern of faith under fire surfaces in Hebrews 11, a chapter some have labeled "The Faith Hall of Fame." There, the author records in grim detail the trials that may befall faith-full people, concluding, "The world was not worthy of them." Hebrews adds this intriguing evaluation of its impressive assemblage: "Therefore God is not ashamed to be called their God." For me, that phrase puts a reverse spin on Dorothy Sayers' remark about God's humiliations — the church has borne God shame, yes, but it has also brought him moments of pride, and the gaunt saints of Hebrews 11 demonstrate how.

Saints become saints by somehow clinging to the stubborn conviction that God deserves our trust, even when it looks like the world is caving in. The saints of Hebrews 11 placed their hope in a better country, a heavenly one, and for that reason God was not ashamed to be called their God. Paradoxically, faith develops best amid uncertainty and confusion — if you doubt that, read for yourself the life stories of the people recorded there. God's favorites, *especially* God's favorites, are not immune from times of testing. As Paul Tournier said, "Where there is no longer any opportunity for doubt, there is no longer any opportunity for faith either."

When I finished my study of God's favorites, one fact stood out above all others. Those people hardly resembled the healthy, prosperous, pampered saints I hear described on religious television. The contrast was striking, and it puzzled me for a time. Perhaps here is the difference: religious television must concern itself with pleasing an audience of thousands, even millions. God's favorites are singularly devoted to pleasing an audience of just One.

To be commanded to love God at all, let alone in the wilderness, is like being commanded to be well when we are sick, to sing for joy when we are dying of thirst, to run when our legs are broken. But this is the first and great commandment nonetheless. Even in the wilderness — especially in the wilderness — you shall love him.

(Frederick Buechner)

King David's Spiritual Secret

Author Joseph Heller *(Catch 22, Good as Gold)* once tried his hand at retelling the life of King David. The resulting book, *God Knows,* met with little success, and a *Time* magazine reviewer suggested the reason: no novelization could improve on the Bible's spicy account of King David's life. Biblical history does not omit any of the seamy parts, but lays out all the lies and deceits, the endless battles, the acts of bravado, the feigned insanity, the family failures, the adultery, the murder.

Heller's mildly irreverent book about David does raise a question, though, an unavoidable question that stalks the biblical record as well. How could a person so obviously flawed become known as "a man after God's own heart"? For a time in Israel, Jehovah was called "the

God of David"; the identification between the two was that close. What was David's secret?

I completed a reading exercise that just may offer a clue. I compared, to use the current jargon, David's inward journey with his outward journey. The Book of Psalms, notably its seventy-three poems attributed to David, offers a window into his soul. Some of those seventy-three have introductory comments revealing the actual circumstances in which they were written. I decided to read from David's spiritual diary of psalms first and then, from the evidence of that "inner" record, try to imagine what "outer" events prompted such words. Then I turned to the historical account in the books of Samuel and compared my inventions with what had actually taken place.

Psalm 56 includes the famous words, "In God I trust"; in it David gratefully credits God for delivering his soul from death and his feet from stumbling. Just reading the psalm, it sounded to me as if God had miraculously intervened and rescued David from some predicament. But what actually happened? When I turned to 1 Samuel 21, I read the story of a scared prisoner who drooled spittle and flung himself about like a madman in a desperate attempt to save his own neck. There was no miracle, so far as I could see — just a canny renegade with strong survival instincts.

Next, I read Psalm 59: "O my strength, I sing praise to you; you, O God, are my fortress, my loving God." Once again it seemed from the psalm that God had intervened to save David's life. But in 1 Samuel 19, the corresponding passage, I read of a chase scene: David snuck out through a window while his wife threw off the pursuers by wrapping a statue in goats' hair. Once more, David's psalm had given God all the credit for what looked like human ingenuity.

Psalm 57 introduces a new tone, of weakness and trembling. It shows a fugitive crying out for mercy. David's faith was wavering when he wrote that psalm, I guessed. But when I looked up the historical account in 1 Samuel 24 I found one of the most extraordinary displays of defiant courage in all of history.

Psalm 18 gives a summary of David's entire military career. Written when he was undisputed king at last, it recalls in incandescent detail the many miracles of deliverance from God. If you read just that psalm, and not the background history, you would think David lived a particularly charmed and sheltered life. The psalm tells nothing of the years on the run, the all-night battles, the chase scenes, and the wily escape plots that fill the pages of 1 and 2 Samuel.

In short, if you read the psalms attributed to David and then try to envision his life, you will fail miserably. You might imagine a pious, other-worldly hermit, or a timid, neurotic soul favored by God, but not a giant of strength and valor. What can explain the disparity between two biblical records, of David's inward and outward journeys?

*   *   *

We all experience both an inner life and an outer life simultaneously. We perceive life as a kind of movie, consisting of characters and sets and twists of plot — with ourselves playing the starring roles. If I attend the same event as you (say, a party) I will take home similar "outer" facts about what happened and who was there, but a wholly different "inner" point of view. My memory will dwell on what impression I made. Was I witty or charming? Did I offend someone, or embarrass myself? Did I look good to others? Most likely, you will ask the same questions, but about yourself.

David, however, seemed to view life a little differently. His exploits — killing wild animals bare-handed, felling Goliath, surviving Saul's onslaughts, routing the Philistines — surely earned him a starring role. But as he reflected on those events, and wrote poems about them, he found a way to make Yahweh, God of Israel, the one on center stage. Whatever the phrase "practicing the presence of God" means, David experienced. Whether he expressed that presence in lofty poems of praise, or in an earthy harangue, in either case he intentionally involved God in the details of his life.

David had confidence that he mattered to God. After one narrow escape he wrote, "[God] rescued me because he delighted in me" (Ps. 18:19). Another time he argued, in so many words (Ps. 30), "What good will it do you if I die, Lord? Who will praise you then?" And when David felt betrayed by God, he let him know. It was he, after all, who first spoke the words, "My God, my God, why have you forsaken me?" He called God into account, demanding that God keep up his end of their special relationship.

Throughout his life David believed, truly believed, that the invisible world of God, heaven, and the angels was every bit as real as his own world of swords and spears and caves and thrones. The psalms form a record of his conscious effort to subject his own daily life to the reality of that invisible world beyond him.

Psalm 57 illustrates this process as well as any. David composed it, the title says, when he had fled from Saul into a cave. 1 Samuel 24 sets the scene: Saul with his well-armed hordes had completely encircled David's small band. Blocked off from all escape, David holed up in a cave next to a sheep pen. The psalm expresses anxiety and fear, of course. But it ends with an oddly triumphant imperative, "Be exalted, O God, above the heavens; let your glory be over all the earth." Somehow, in the process of writing, David was able to lift his eyes from the dank, smelly cave to the heavens above. In the most unlikely of settings, he came to affirm, simply, "God reigns."

Perhaps it was the next morning that David strode out, unarmed, and confronted King Saul's entire army with no weapon but an appeal to conscience. Perhaps the very process of writing the psalm had emboldened him for such a bravura display of moral courage.

Few of us, thankfully, live on the edge of mortal danger, as David did. But we do, like David, have times when nerves fail, when fear creeps in, when it seems that God has withdrawn, when hostile forces have us surrounded. At such a moment I turn to the Psalms. I have a sneaking suspicion that David wrote psalms as a form of spiritual therapy, a way of "talking himself into" faith when his spirit and emotions were wavering. And now, centuries later, we can use those very same prayers as steps of faith, a path to lead us from an obsession with ourselves to the actual presence of our God.

Part VI

Another World

Why do science and theology have such a hard time getting along?

Is there really an "invisible world" out there? If so, what difference does it make?

Why do people show great interest in "near-death experiences" but no interest in heaven?

Why do people show great interest in "near-death experiences" but little interest in death experiences?

How much space in the Bible is devoted to the Crucifixion and how much to the Resurrection? Shouldn't the allotment be the other way around?

If the Resurrection had occurred on network television, would the whole world now believe in Jesus? What would make the whole world believe in Jesus?

What should a Christian look like? What should a Christian smell like?

Beware Black Holes

Theology and science have had a tenuous relationship ever since Galileo and Copernicus. In some ways Christianity has never quite recovered from the cosmological revolution, which displaced humankind from the center of the universe and shunted us off to an insignificant outpost. Perhaps because of this hunker-down posture toward science, few current Christian thinkers seem to be taking advantage of remarkable developments in modern physics. In their own way, Einstein and Bohr accomplished a revolution every bit as momentous as Copernicus's, though in shocking new directions.

To begin with, not merely humankind but individual men and women have, through modern physics, regained their place as central figures in the history of universe.

For if modern physics has taught us anything, it is that the conscious individual is an essential component in, well, *everything*. In Newtonian physics, individuals have no special place in the universe except as occasional participants in the orderly world of cause and effect. But some twentieth-century scientists assert that the very reality of an occurrence depends upon whether an observer is present.

As Bernard D'Espagnat says in *Scientific American*, "The doctrine that the world is made up of objects whose existence is independent of human consciousness turns out to be in conflict with quantum mechanics and with facts established by experiment." In other words, he questions whether anything even *exists* apart from consciousness. At the very least, the individual matters, and the observer plays an essential role. More poetic physicists spout proverbs such as, "If you cut a blade of grass you shake the universe."

The average layman quickly loses footing in the Alice-in-Wonderland realm of relativity and quantum physics. We learn that our favorite chair is formed of great gaping spaces and a few unpredictable atoms spinning around; but still we treat it as a solid object by sitting on it. We learn that time varies depending on gravitation and movement, and that an astronaut twin who rockets out into space can come back thirty-six years younger than his brother; yet still we rely on watches to get us to the office on time. This whole bewildering world of modern physics, with its blackboard-length equations and its creepy terms like worm-holes, antimatter, quantum foam, and black holes, seems better left alone. With a few exceptions here or there, you can get along fine depending on trusty old Newton.

And yet Christians must not flee modern physics so quickly. Many of its main tenets about the nature of time and space have been verified by enterprising scientists who bounce lasers off the moon, photograph stars during solar eclipses, and fly atomic clocks around the world in jumbo jets. We can't just ignore the results of these experiments. What's more, the remarkable discoveries being bruited about with childlike astonishment offer new constructs for understanding some elusive theological doctrines.

Consider one such doctrine: the timelessness of God. For thousands of years Christians have cited proverbs such as "A thousand years is as a day in God's sight," to express their belief that God somehow views time differently. He is *outside* time and space, we say. We see human history as a sequential series of still-frames, one by one, as in a motion picture; but God sees the entire movie at once, in a flash. Although Christians cite this belief and nearly all theologians since Augustine have discussed it, who could comprehend it?

Enter modern physics. Time, we are now told, depends on movement and the observer's relative position. Take a very primitive example. When I glance in the sky at 3:12 in the afternoon, I see a bright star, the sun, that hangs in space some ninety-three million miles away. The light actually left that star 500 seconds ago, and traveled at the rate of 186,000 miles per second to reach me. As an observer on earth, I look into the sky at 3:12 p.m., although I dimly realize that I am viewing the astral results of what took place at 3:04 p.m. earth time. If the sun suddenly vanished in a sneak attack by a voracious black hole, I would not know it for eight minutes. Then the sky would darken, and I would cry "The sun is gone!" and prepare for extinction.

Imagine now a very large person — I mean *very* large, someone with a legspan of at least, say, ninety-three million miles. This person stands in our solar system with his left foot planted firmly on earth and his right foot (asbestos-wrapped) resting on the sun. Suddenly, the person stamps his right foot. Immediately, solar flares shoot out in all directions and the sun belches gases. Eight minutes later I, on earth, will notice the dramatic change in the sun.

But I am trapped on earth. The very large person exists partially on earth and partially on the sun — his consciousness spans both. Although he is partly standing on earth, he has knowledge of the stomping right foot eight minutes in advance of anyone else on earth. A question: "What time is it for the large person?" It depends on the perspective. Take a further mental leap and imagine a Being as large as the universe. He exists simultaneously on earth and on a star in the Andromeda galaxy billions of miles away. If a star explodes in that galaxy, this Being takes note of it immediately, yet he will also "see" it from the viewpoint of an observer on earth millions of years later *as if it has just happened.*

The analogy is inexact, for it traps such a Being in space even as it frees him from time. But it may illustrate how our "first A happens, then B happens" conception of time expresses the very limited perspective of our planet. God, outside both time and space, can view what happens on earth in a way we can only guess at. Such thinking sheds new light on the ancient debates over omniscience, foreknowledge, free will, and determinism.

A word like "foreknowledge" makes sense only when considered from our earth-bound viewpoint. It presumes that time proceeds sequentially, frame by frame. From God's viewpoint, encompassing all of the universe at once, the word has considerably different meaning. Strictly speaking, God does not "foresee" us doing things. He simply *sees* us doing them, in an eternal present.

Timelessness is only one of many doctrines illuminated by contemporary physics. Budding theologians would do well to study the theory of parallel universes as they investigate the problem of evil; the theory of the interconnectedness of all matter and energy as they explore the Bible's words on the union of believers; the theory of how consciousness affects matter as they contemplate the power of prayer. Most of us will need qualified scientist-guides to comprehend these esoterica. Zen Buddhists have seized the day and published volumes on how their beliefs match up with contemporary models of the universe. I hope we don't lag too far behind. Religious faith, like matter, is in constant peril of being swallowed by black holes.

Born-Again Mathematics

I do not know how to phrase this delicately, so I will just come out and say it: I'm a bit worried about the mathematical aptitude shown in the Bible. Frederick Buechner goes so far as to call it "atrocious." I know that kind of statement gets some people riled up, but the more I look the more I understand what he means. Consider the evidence for yourself — an example from each Gospel, just to be mathematically precise.

Matthew 20. This chapter opens with a parable I hear few sermons preached on, with good reason. It contradicts all known laws of fairness, human motivation, and just compensation. Briefly, Jesus tells of a farmer who hires people to work his fields. Some punch in at sunrise, some at morning coffee break, some at lunchtime, some at afternoon coffee break, and some an hour before quitting time. Everyone seems grateful for employment, until payroll time, when the stalwarts who worked all through the day under a blazing sun learn that the sweatless upstarts who put in barely an hour get the exact same pay! Anyone who has worked in the fields for a full day can easily identify with their outrage. The boss's decision defies good economics.

I realize that Jesus told this parable as a lesson not on employee benefits, but on God's attitude toward us. But the mathematics seem just as odd in the spiritual realm. The upstarts in this parable remind me of the thief on the cross: a good-for-nothing who barely sneaks in under the wire and yet apparently gets the same reward as someone who has lived a lifetime of devotion and piety. Tales of last-minute forgiveness have a certain winsome quality, to be sure, but such stories will hardly motivate people to live good Christian lives. How would you feel if you were raised in an upright family, attended Christian schools, matured, and established an exemplary home in the community, only to find that some Johnny-come-lately with a deathbed confessional edges you out on Judgment Day?

Mark 12. Here Jesus deals with economics not in parable form but in direct commentary on an act the IRS now labels "Charitable Contribution." A widow drops two coins in the temple collection bucket, an amount worth a mere fraction of a penny. Jesus, who had just been observing rich people contribute sizable investments to the charitable cause, comes up with this statement, "I tell you the truth, this poor widow has put more into the treasury than all the others." I hope he said it softly!

Admiring a widow's motives is one thing, but to follow
with a bewildering — and potentially offensive — mathematical assertion like that!

Perhaps we can excuse Jesus' comments on the basis
that certain important rules of fund-raising had not yet
been discovered. Surely it took time for the New Testament church to break away from the legalistic practice of
tithing and adjust to free-will offerings and their diplo-
matic requirements (James 2, for example, shows a shocking disregard for fund-raising principles). And not until
our present time have we seen such breakthrough innova-
tions as personalized letters, leather-bound premiums,
"inner circle" contributors' clubs, and fund-raising ban-
quets (where the widow would doubtless feel out of
place). Sentimentality for a widow's faithfulness certainly
must not interfere with "relationship building" and
"donor maintenance" of more substantial contributors —
that would be bad mathematics indeed.

Luke 15. We all know this story, of the noble shepherd
who left his flock of 99 and plunged into the darkness to
search for one lost sheep. A nice homily, agreed, but reflect
for a moment on the underlying mathematics. Jesus says
the shepherd left the 99 sheep "in the country," which
presumably means vulnerable to rustlers, wolves, or a
feral desire to bolt free down some path. How would the
shepherd feel if he returned with the one lost lamb slung
across his shoulders only to find 24 others now missing?

Fortunately, the science of church growth now in-
structs us to invest our resources in those activities that
benefit the greatest number of people. Because homo-
geneous groups work so much better, chasing after social
deviants amounts to bad stewardship. Obviously, the one

sheep left the flock because he did not fit in, or perhaps wanted to enjoy his own freedom — hardly a reason to endanger the whole flock.

John 12. One of Jesus' best friends, Mary (who had already demonstrated dubious standards of time efficiency), earns a place in history for her lack of astuteness in economics. She takes a pint — a *pint!* A year's wages! — of perfume and pours it on Jesus' feet. Just thinking about this outlandish act raises my blood pressure. Would not an ounce accomplish the same purpose? Did Jesus really want perfume spilled all over his feet? And even Judas, albeit with mixed motives, can see the pure wastefulness of the act: think of all the poor people who could have been helped by the treasure now running in rivulets across the dirt floor.

The New Testament view of mathematics reminds me of a parable by Kierkegaard (another questionable mathematician). He tells of a vandal who breaks into a department store at night and does not steal anything but rather rearranges all the price tags. The next day shopkeepers, not to mention the delighted customers, encounter such oddities as diamond necklaces on sale for a dollar and cheap costume-jewelry earrings costing thousands. The gospel is like that, says Kierkegaard: it changes around all our normal assumptions about worth and value.

Whatever Happened to Heaven?

A strange fact about modern American life: although 71 percent of us claim to believe in an afterlife, no one much talks about it. I once looked up "Heaven" in one of Chicago's largest university libraries and found that the previous four annual volumes of the *Reader's Guide to Periodical Literature* recorded a grand total of zero articles on the subject. I found many articles concerning old age, many about death, some on out-of-the-body experiences, but none about heaven.

Surely, I thought, this dearth simply reflects the bias of secular culture. But even when I looked in the *Religion Index One: Periodicals*, I could locate only a handful of articles on heaven: three, for instance, during the years 1981-1982 (and one of those was in French). To me, that seems truly odd. Although percentages don't apply to eternity, assume for the sake of argument that 99 percent of our existence will take place in heaven. Isn't it bizarre that we simply ignore heaven, acting as if it doesn't matter? Several fine books have emerged in recent years against this trend, but they hardly fill the void.

As recently as the nineteenth century, publishers churned out serious thousand-page anthologies of poetic and prose imaginings of heaven. Now we get most of our images of heaven from *New Yorker* cartoons and from jokes about St. Peter at the Pearly Gate. What happened? Karl Menninger raised a pertinent theological question with his book *Whatever Became of Sin?* Well, the demise of heaven causes me at least equal concern. How did it simply vanish from modern consciousness? After giving the subject some thought, I have come up with three suggestions that may help explain the mystery.

1. Affluence has brought us *in this life* what former generations could only anticipate in heaven. In the developed countries, a majority of citizens now have plentiful food, a relief from pain, and surroundings of beauty and luxury. The biblical promise of such a state has lost some of its luster.

Even those who lack such comfort focus their energies almost exclusively on getting it in this life. Karl Marx dubbed religion the "opiate of the people" because it dangled a promise of "pie in the sky" before the lower classes, thus dulling their desire for material satisfaction now.* Marx's critique sounds quaint today. Who is prom-

---

*I have sometimes wondered how Marx, a Jew, fit in this theory with his knowledge of the Old Testament. God revealed grand and elaborate

ising pie in the sky anymore? Religious organizations
such as the World Council of Churches and evangelical
relief agencies instead encourage us to redistribute the pie
here on earth.

   2. A creeping paganism invites us to accept death as
the culmination of life on earth, not as a violent transition
into an ongoing life. Elisabeth Kübler-Ross (who happens
to believe in an afterlife) defined five stages of death, with
the implicit suggestion that the "Acceptance" stage is the
most healthful and appropriate. I have watched in hospital therapy groups as dying patients work desperately
toward that state of calm acceptance, thereby overruling
the impulse of instinct and conscience to reject death as
an enemy. Strangely, no one ever talked about heaven in
those groups; it seemed embarrassing, somehow cowardly. What inversion of values has led us to commend a
belief in annihilation as brave and dismiss a hope for
blissful eternity as cowardly?

   3. The older, biblical images of heaven have lost their
appeal. Walls of emerald, sapphire, and jasper, streets of
gold, and gates of pearl may have inspired Middle Eastern peasants, but they don't mean much to the world of
Bauhaus. And religious leaders and artists have failed to
come up with satisfactory new images. What will heaven
be like? A place where "all a body would have to do was
to go around all day long with a harp and sing, forever

---

truths about the nature of a just society, going so far as to carve out a
nation to embody those principles. Yet the Old Testament gives very
few glimpses of an afterlife. It almost seems as if God waited through
a few thousand years of human history without spelling out eternal
rewards in order to forestall human distortions like a "pie in the sky"
approach to justice.

and ever," sounds as unattractive to most of us as it did to Huck Finn. It seems to me Christian communicators have a clear responsibility to project a new understanding of heaven into modern consciousness. If we fail, we forfeit one of our faith's greatest features.

To people who are trapped in pain, in broken homes, in economic chaos, in hatred and fear, in violence — to these, heaven offers the promise of a time, far longer and more substantial than this time on earth, of health and wholeness and pleasure and peace. If we do not believe that, then, as the Apostle Paul noted in 1 Corinthians 15, there's not much reason for being a Christian in the first place. And if we do believe, it should change our lives. I say that because I have seen the electrifying results that can happen when the idea of heaven comes alive.

My wife Janet once worked with senior citizens near a Chicago housing project judged the poorest community in the United States. About half her clients were white, half were black. All of them have lived through harsh times: two world wars, the Great Depression, social upheavals. And all of them, in their seventies and eighties, lived in awareness of death. Yet Janet noted a remarkable difference in the way the whites and the blacks faced death. There were exceptions, of course, but the trend was this: many of the whites became increasingly more fearful and uptight. They complained about their lives, their families, and their deteriorating health. The blacks, in contrast, maintained a good humor and triumphant spirit even though most of them had more apparent reason for bitterness and despair. (Most lived in the South just one generation after slavery, and suffered a lifetime of economic oppression and injustice. They were senior citizens before the first Civil Rights bills were passed.)

What caused the difference in outlooks? Janet concluded the answer is hope, a hope that traced directly to the blacks' bedrock belief in heaven. "This world is not my home, I'm just a passin' through," they sang. These words and others like them ("Swing low, sweet chariot, comin' for to carry me home") came out of a tragic period of history, when everything in this world looked bleak. But somehow black churches managed to instill a vivid belief in a home beyond this one. If you want to hear newer, more relevant images of heaven, attend a few African-American funerals. With characteristic eloquence, the preachers paint word pictures of a life so serene and sensuous that everyone in the congregation starts fidgeting to go there. The mourners feel grief, naturally, but in its proper place: as an interruption, a temporary setback in a battle whose end has already been determined.

Somehow, these neglected saints have learned to anticipate and enjoy God in spite of the difficulties of their lives on earth. When we get to heaven, many of us may be surprised to learn what it means to enjoy God. For others, such as these elderly blacks in the slums of Chicago, that joy will seem more like a long-awaited homecoming than a visit to a new place. Who knows, they may save a few hundred years' awkward transition.

Imagine There's No Heaven

Anthropologists report, with some sheepish bewilderment, that every human society discovered thus far has a belief in an afterlife. Religion specialists — especially those who go by the tongue-cramping name "phenomenologists" — seize upon that fact. They see in such stubborn persistence of belief a "rumor of transcendence," a vestige of our immortal natures.

Reading about the near-universal belief in an afterlife got me thinking in another direction entirely. I started wondering what a society might look like if it *did not* believe in an afterlife. How would the denial of immortality affect everyday life? I let my imagination run, and came up with the following conclusions. For the sake of a convenient label (and with apologies to

215

Samuel Butler, author of *Erehwon*), I'll call my mythical society Acirema.

1. Aciremans value youth above all else. Since for them nothing exists beyond life on earth, youth represents hope. They have no other future to look forward to. As a result, anything preserving the illusion of youthfulness flourishes. Sports is a national obsession. Magazine covers present wrinkle-free faces and gorgeous bodies. The best-selling books and videotapes feature alluring women in their forties who demonstrate exercises that, if followed faithfully, will make you look a decade younger.

2. Naturally, Aciremans do not value old age, for elderly people offer a distasteful reminder of the end of life. Unlike young people, they can never represent hope. The Acireman health industry thus promotes skin creams, cures for baldness, cosmetic surgery, and many other elaborate means of masking the effects of aging, the prelude to death. In especially callous parts of Acirema, citizens even confine the elderly to their own housing, isolated from the general populace.

3. Acirema emphasizes "image" rather than "substance." Such practices as dieting, exercise, and body-building, for example, have attained the status of pagan worship rites. A well-formed body visibly demonstrates achievement in this world, whereas nebulous inner qualities — compassion, self-sacrifice, humility — merit little praise. As an unfortunate side-effect, a disabled or disfigured person, regardless of personal character, has great difficulty competing in Acirema.

4. Acireman religion focuses exclusively on how one fares in the here and now, for there is no reward system after death. Those Aciremans who still believe in a deity

look for God's approval in terms of good health and
prosperity on earth. At one time, Acireman priests
pursued what they called "evangelism," but now they
devote most of their energy to improving the welfare of
fellow citizens.

5. Recently, crime has taken a turn toward the
grotesquely violent and bizarre. In other primitive societies, citizens grow up with a vague fear of eternal judgment hanging over them, but Aciremans have no such
deterrents to deviant behavior.

6. Aciremans spend billions of dollars to maintain
elderly bodies on life-support systems, while at the same
time they permit, even encourage, the abortion of fe-
tuses. This is not as paradoxical as it seems, for
Aciremans believe that human life begins at birth and
ends at death.

7. Until recently, Acireman psychologists had to treat
their patients' atavistic reactions of fear and anger in the
face of death. New techniques, however, have shown
promise in overcoming such primal instincts. Aciremans
are now taught to view "acceptance" as the most mature
response to the perfectly natural state of death. Scholars
have successfully devalued ancient attitudes about dying
in a "noble" manner. For Aciremans, the ideal death is a
peaceful departure during sleep.

8. Acireman scientists are still working to eliminate
the problem of death. In the meantime, most deaths take
place in the presence of trained professionals, in a sealed-
off area. To lessen the shock, euphemisms such as "passing" and "going on" are substituted for the inelegant
word "death." And all ceremonies accompanying death
play down its discontinuity from life. Corpses are pre-

served chemically and stored in airtight, leakproof con-
tainers.

*   *   *

Just thinking about such a society gives me the creeps. I
sure am glad I live in the good ol' U.S.A., where, as
George Gallup assures us, the vast majority of the population believes in an afterlife.

Sunday Afternoon at the Beach

Lifeguards in wooden boats row lazily in place, just enough to counter the gentle swells of Lake Michigan. A plane circles overhead, trailing a promotional streamer for an auto dealership. Sailboats break the abutting blues of the horizon with tiny triangles of white.

On the beach itself, Chicago's ethnic life is splayed out for all to see. Four blocks north, a Latino domain, English is spoken as a second language if at all. Four blocks south lies Oak Street Beach, where Yuppies shed their designer clothes for designer bathing suits. But in between, at North Avenue, the melting pot simmers: macho men on roller skates, decked out in plastic helmets and kneepads, cradling oversized radios; serious cyclists honking for sidewalk space; shiny, sinewy bodies on display at a volleyball court. More bodies, gorgeous bodies stretched out in a random pattern on the beach, ironically call to mind one of those staged reenactments of the horror of Hiroshima. These, however — with strips of cloth cut high over the hips, tops unfastened — are taking their radiation in slow, buttery doses.

A few disgruntled sun worshipers mutter curse words and move away from a knot of fifty people gathered by the water's edge. Near the "sixth light pole north of North Avenue," a ceremony is about to begin. These too wear bathing suits, though not quite so skimpy. They are from LaSalle Street Church in downtown Chicago, and they have come for a baptism. The warmup songs, "Amazing Grace" and a few others, sound thin, no match for the surrounding ghetto blasters.

Thirteen baptismal candidates line up to speak, probing the sand with their feet in search of cooler strata. The others strain to catch their words. There are two young stockbrokers, married, who want to "identify with Christ more publicly." A woman of Cuban descent speaks, dressed all in white. A tall, bronzed man says he was an agnostic until six months ago. An aspiring opera singer admits she just decided to seek baptism this morning, and asks for prayer because she hates cold water. (The air temperature is 93 degrees; Lake Michigan is 55.)

An 85-year-old black woman has asked to be immersed despite her doctor's advice ("Strangest request I ever heard," he said). A real estate investor, a pregnant woman, a med student, and a few others each take a turn explaining why they are here today, standing in a lineup on North Avenue Beach. One of the candidates has converted to Christianity from a Hindu-type cult in Berkeley,

California. To the passersby — the dog-walkers, the cops, the strutting bodies — the baptism service itself must seem cultic. Hymns and prayers are rarely heard on Sunday afternoon at the beach.

The candidates respond to a liturgy:

"Do you renounce Satan and all the spiritual forces of wickedness that rebel against God?"

"I renounce them."

"Do you renounce the evil powers of this world which corrupt and destroy the creatures of God?"

"I renounce them."

"Do you renounce all sinful desires that draw you from the love of God?"

"I renounce them."

Some affirmations follow. After all has been renounced and all affirmed, they go, two by two, into the water. Their legs sprout goosebumps by the third step. The pastor waits, waist deep, rocking slightly back and forth with the waves. His mouth moves before each immersion, but we on the shore cannot hear the words. A Frisbee floats past his head. A baptismal candidate swims for it and tosses it back.

The bodies are dipped, quickly. Frosty Lake Michigan makes a memorable impression on the baptized ones: as they emerge from the water, they tremble. Their hair is plastered down, their eyes bright and large from the cold. Back on shore, they get hugs. Wet spots soon appear on all our chests. "Welcome to the Body of Christ," some say.

How different from the baptismal scene that opens Mark's Gospel, I think. We have skyscrapers, not desert rocks, at our backs. Residents of Jerusalem traveled to

John the Baptist's performance — some to believe, some to see the show. We, however, are intruding, taking the ritual into the center, into the city. In our setting, would John have yelled something provocative and gotten himself arrested? But we live in a tolerant country, and no one gets arrested. At most, we elicit stares and bemused smiles. We're not harming anybody. Just another weird religious group.

After an hour, we all leave. The scene at North Avenue Beach goes on, filling in the space our church group had occupied by the water's edge. Our footprints are washed away, our sand redoubt now covered with towels and sunbathers. At the site where new believers renounced Satan and evil, children now form sand castles.

One thought lingers. As each baptismal candidate was presented, someone from the church prayed aloud for that person as he or she began a new walk with God. One, in his prayer, quoted Jesus' promise that great rejoicing breaks out in heaven when a sinner repents. Seen from the lifeguard tower at North Avenue Beach, not much happened that Sunday afternoon. Seen from another viewpoint, that of eternity, a celebration sprang to life that will never end.

Disturbing the Universe

This little babe so few days old
is come to rifle Satan's fold.
All hell doth at his presence quake
though He Himself for cold do shake.

— Robert Southwell (16th century)

Birth

At most, a handful of shepherds witnessed the drama of the birth night. Think of it: The Incarnation, which sliced history into two parts (a fact even our calendars grudgingly acknowledge), had more animal than human witnesses.

There was indeed a murmur of eucatastrophe, a sudden burst of grandeur. The universe could not let the Visit go unannounced, and for an instant the sky grew luminous with angels. All Hollywood special effects crews would fall dazzled before such a scene. Yet who saw it then? Illiterate peasants who failed to leave their names.

Death

Calvary was less visibly spectacular. The miracle then lay not in what happened but what did not. The ugly ritual of violence played itself out with no interference. Angels stayed away that day, held off by the Son of God himself. Even the Father turned his back, or so it surely seemed. He, too, let history take its course, let all that was wrong with the world triumph over all that was right.

"He saved others; let him save himself," they jeered. This time, this public moment when God appeared downright helpless, the cameras of history were rolling, recording it all. Large crowds watched every excruciating detail of trial, verdict, crucifixion, and death. No one could claim that Jesus did not die.

Afterdeath

When the Miracle of Miracles occurred, only a couple witnesses stood by: coarse Roman guards, the forgotten men of Easter. They and only they saw with human eyes the stunning scene of the impossible made possible.

Showing an incurably human reflex, they immediately ran to the authorities to report the disturbance.

Later that afternoon, the resurrection seemed rather hazy and remote — not nearly as significant as, say, the stacks of freshly minted silver before them. Do we ever wonder at the fact that the eyewitnesses of that great day died apparent unbelievers?

*   *   *

Christmas, Good Friday, Easter: those three days are marked on the calendars of half the world. Despite bribes paid the Roman guards and an elaborate cover-up conspiracy, word got out. A glimmer of faith took hold, and takes hold still.

People sometimes fault God for not making faith any easier, for not making himself more obvious. Another look at those three momentous days may shed light on this puzzle of faith. The first event, Christ's birth, seemed a scandal to all but a few insiders and ragtag guests. The last event, the resurrection, went unobserved but by two, who quickly edited their accounts. Only the middle event, the crucifixion, took place in public, for all the world to see.

How to account for the significance of the cross? It hardly seemed "miraculous" at the time. What could be more mundane than another dreary execution by Roman occupation troops? Even now the memorial day, Good Friday, can slip quietly by, unobserved, a mere prelude to the cymbal sounds of Easter.

Yet from the cosmos, from the view, say, of an angel just beyond Andromeda, Good Friday was the most surprising miracle of all. The Incarnation was unique, of course, but it had faint parallels. Celestial beings had slipped in and out of time zones before — remember Jacob's wrestler, Abraham's visitors. As for the resurrection, a few humans had roused from the dead in Old Testament times, and Jesus had clearly proved his mastery over death (ask Lazarus). But when the Son of God himself died on Planet Earth — nothing like that had happened before or will happen again. Nature itself seemed to convulse: the ground shook, tombs cracked open, the sky went black.

More than death died that Friday afternoon. The Apostle Paul said about that day, "And having disarmed the powers and authorities, he made a public spectacle of them, triumphing over them by the cross" (Col. 2:15). A public spectacle it was, when Christ exposed the very powers and authorities that men and women stake their lives on. The most advanced religion of the day judged him guilty, and the most advanced government carried out the sentence. Satan's grand design, hatched in Eden, was accomplished in the name of piety and justice and law. Christ triumphed by exposing those powers and authorities as false gods who could never keep their lofty promises.

The crucifixion forever set Christ's followers against the powers of this world. "Jews demand miraculous signs and Greeks look for wisdom," said Paul, "but we preach Christ crucified: a stumbling block to Jews and foolishness to Gentiles" (1 Cor. 1:22-23). Not much has changed in two thousand years. Today it's the scientists who demand signs and the politicians who look for wisdom; and now, as then, the cross looms as a stumbling block of faith.

The three events — birth, death, and resurrection — were surely tremors in the cosmos. Yet, carried out so mysteriously, with such a strange assortment of witnesses, they forever complicated faith. They gave just enough reason to believe for those who, like the disciples, chose faith, and just enough reason not to believe for those who, like the Roman guards, chose doubt. That, too, hasn't changed since Jesus' time.

The Fragrant Season

The year before the PTL scandal broke, I heard Tammy Faye Bakker say something that troubled me, but I wasn't sure why. She stared out from my television screen, her long, dark eyelashes coated with what *The Wittenburg Door* once cattily described as "industrial strength mascara." "Ooh!" she gushed, "The Christian life is just *sooo* great that I think I would become a Christian even if it wasn't true!" She had just been interviewing people with inspiring stories and yes, Tammy Faye, the Christian life as described on the air did sound pretty great. But although I was touched by her enthusiasm, something about her declaration — ". . . even if it wasn't true" — bothered me. It seemed somehow wrong, but I couldn't put my finger on the problem.

I finally located the source of my discomfort in
1 Corinthians 15, the Bible's central chapter on resurrection from the dead. There, the apostle Paul stakes his faith
on the *truth* of Jesus' resurrection. With remarkable blunt-
ness he argues that if Christ had not been raised, his own
preaching would be useless, as would our faith. Further-
more, he adds, except for the resurrection "we are to be
pitied more than all men."

Paul, not known for his timidity, nevertheless admits
he would never risk his life for a faith with no basis in
truth. Why endanger himself? It would hardly be worth
fighting wild beasts in Ephesus for a phantom faith. He-
donism offers a far more attractive alternative, and Paul
candidly proposes that, "If the dead are not raised, let us
eat and drink, for tomorrow we die." (Unlike many television evangelists, Paul seemed to expect from the Christian life, not health and wealth, but a measure of suffering.
He told Timothy, "In fact, everyone who wants to live a
godly life in Christ Jesus will be persecuted.")

As I read Paul's reflections on his hardships, I could
not imagine him agreeing with Tammy Faye's assessment
of the Christian life. I also caught myself wondering
whether Tammy Faye could make the same statement
today, with just as much enthusiasm.

*   *   *

Later, long after I saw Tammy Faye on television, I came
across yet another intriguing passage in Paul's writings.
Two sentences bring together the upbeat exuberance of
Tammy Faye's guests and the blunt realism of 1 Corinthians 15. Paul wrote to the church in Corinth, "For we are

to God the aroma of Christ among those who are being
saved and those who are perishing. To the one, we are
the smell of death; to the other, the fragrance of life"
(2 Cor. 2:15-16).

According to Paul, the same fragrance can convey
vastly different aromas, depending on the nose. To the
unbelieving world our faith has the redolence of death
about it. It intrudes with an unsettling reminder of mor-
tality, and of another world that sits in judgment on this
one. Among unbelievers, personal examples of denial and
sacrificial love may provoke begrudging admiration for
"the Christian ethic." But, as Paul said, undiluted he-
donism has far more appeal. Think about what attracts a
receptive audience in America: billionaires and movie
stars write hugely successful biographies, but I have yet
to see a best-seller about an inner-city pastor. And the
occasional PBS documentary on a Christian "saint" like
Mother Teresa can hardly compete with "Wheel of Fortune" or "Melrose Place." To the one, we are the smell of
death. That smell hung like a cloud over Mother Teresa
— literally, for it was among the dying that she chose to
serve Christ. Her religious order even now is opening
hospices for AIDS patients.

The wisdom of the Cross appears foolish to the
world, and Paul confessed it would appear foolish to him
too were it not for an event that occurred two days after
the crucifixion. Believers — those people convinced that
the resurrection really happened — gain, so to speak, a
new set of olfactory receptors. Beyond the stench of Good
Friday they can detect the startling fragrance of new life.
For this reason, and this reason only, the Christian faith
is worth pursuing. To extend Paul's argument, if there is

no resurrection, why restrain sexual or even violent urges? Why care about the poor and deformed? Why seek humility and servanthood while others seek ego strokes? Why give money away when you can hoard it? Such a life is to be pitied, not envied. It gives off the aroma of death — to all but those with sanctified noses.

*   *   *

I write this at the beginning of spring, the fragrant season, a time of great rejoicing to those of us who live in northern cities. For too long I have walked past dirty snowpiles that serve as traps for dog droppings, litter, and particles of automobile exhaust. Now the ground is growing soft again, and even on the vacant lots of Chicago the rich fragrance of earth is breaking free. Spring is on the way, its approach heralded by a thousand scents. The dense sweet smell of lilacs will soon grace the grim alley behind my home. In a few months, roses will overtake all other scents there. And then will come the pungent aroma of honeysuckle that never fails to transport me back to boyhood hikes in the Georgia woods.

By no accident the church calendar, too, is approaching a fragrant season; early celebrants of Easter combined remembrance of the earth's resurrection with that of Christ's. I think again of Paul's metaphor of smell: "For we are to God the aroma of Christ among those who are being saved and those who are perishing. To the one, we are the smell of death; to the other, the fragrance of life." The aroma of death never fully dissipates. We die daily, said Paul, and our acts of self-denial will surely seem morbid, even masochistic to some. But beyond that fragrance is the springlike scent of new life, and the only path that leads there is the path of the Cross.

A smell, any smell, is a mere hint, a gaseous announcement of something more substantial. And that is why we can be to God the aroma of Christ. Because of Easter, and only because of Easter, his fragrance becomes ours.

Listen, Christians. Can you hear the sound of laughter from the other side of death? Breathe deeply of a fragrance like no other. Let it fill your lungs this spring, this Easter.